OCT   2003

SKIING

Titles in the History of Sports series include:
- Baseball
- Basketball
- Cycling
- Football
- Golf
- Hockey
- Soccer
- Tennis
- Track and Field
- Volleyball
- Wrestling

HISTORY OF SPORTS

SKIING

BY ALISON COTTER

LUCENT BOOKS®

THOMSON

GALE

San Diego • Detroit • New York • San Francisco • Cleveland • New Haven, Conn. • Waterville, Maine • London • Munich

On Cover: Picabo Street soars through the air to a first place
finish at a World Cup downhill race in 1994.

LIBRARY OF CONGRESS CATALOGING-IN-PUBLICATION DATA

Cotter, Alison, 1963–
    Skiing / by Alison Cotter.
        p. cm.—(History of Sports)
Summary: Discusses the origins and evolution of skiing, including different styles, equipment, and techniques, as well as memorable events and key personalities in the sport's
history.
Includes bibliographical references (p. 97–100) and index.
    ISBN 1-59018-072-0 (hardback : alk. paper)
    1. Skis and skiing—Juvenile literature. [1. Skis and skiing.] I. Title. II. Series.
    GV854.315 .C68 2003
    796.93—dc21

                                  2002006976

Printed in the United States of America

Contents

FOREWORD

MORE THAN MANY areas of human endeavor, sports give us the opportunity to see the possibilities in our physical selves. As participants, we all too quickly find limits to how fast we can run, how high we can jump, how far and straight we can hit a golf ball. But as spectators we can surpass those limits as we view the accomplishments of others and see how fast, how smooth, and how strong a human being can be. We marvel at the gravity-defying leaps of a Michael Jordan as he strains toward a basketball hoop or at the dribbling of a Mia Hamm as she eludes defenders on the soccer field. We shake our heads in disbelief at the talents of a young Tiger Woods hitting an approach shot to the green or the speed of a Carl Lewis as he appears to glide around an Olympic track.

These are what the sports media call "the oohs and ahhs" of sports—the stuff of highlight reels and *Sports Illustrated* covers. But to understand a sport only in the context of its most artistic modern athletes is shortsighted, for it does little justice to the accomplishments of the athletes or to the sport itself. Far more wise is to view a sport as a continuum—a constantly moving, evolving process. On this continuum are not only the superstars of today, but the people who first played the sport, who thought about rules and strategies that would make it more challenging to play as well as a delight to watch.

Lucent Books' series, *The History of Sports*, provides such a continuum. Each book explores the development of a sport from its basic roots onward, and tries to answer questions that a reader might wonder about. Who were its first players, and what sorts of rules did the sport have then? What kinds of equipment were used in the beginning and what changes have taken place over the years?

Each title in *The History of Sports* also identifies key individuals in the sport's history—people whose leadership or skills have made a difference in the way the sport is played today. Included will be the easily recognized names, the Mia Hamms and the Sammy Sosas, the Wilt Chamberlains and the Wilma Rudolphs. But there are also the names of past greats, people like baseball's King Kelly, soccer's Sir Stanley Matthews, and basketball's Hank Luisetti—who may be less familiar today, but were as synonymous with their sports at one time as the "oohs and ahhs" players of today.

Finally, the series looks at the aspects of a sport that are particularly important in its current point on the continuum. Baseball today is better understood knowing about salary caps and union negotiators. One cannot truly know modern soccer without knowing about the specter of fan violence at matches. And learning about the role of instant replay is critical to a thorough understanding of today's professional football games. In viewing a sport as a continuum, the strides that have been made along the way are that much more admirable. It is a richer view, and one that shows how yesterday's limits have been surpassed—and how the limits of today are the possibilities of athletes in the future.

A Sport for the Body and Soul

IN NORWAY, SKIING was a way of life before skiing was ever considered a sport. Today, the sport of skiing is enjoyed by millions in ski resorts and backwoods around the globe. What attracts millions of people to the sport is what ski legend Jean-Claude Killy, in the introduction to John Samuel's book *The Love of Skiing*, calls a combination of exercise and relaxation. That sentiment was held by the Norwegians as far back as the 1800s. They idealized skiing and believed that it improved both the body and the soul. Fridtjof Nansen of Oslo, Norway, captured that sentiment in his 1890 account of his cross-country trek through Greenland. In it, he claimed that being on skis surrounded by nature had the ability to wash civilization from the mind.

It is no surprise then that today skiing has become the pastime of choice for weekenders and vacationers. Killy echoes Nansen when he says that the sport can provide both young and old with an escape from their day-to-day jobs and chores. However, history has labeled Nansen an adventurer, whereas Killy, winner of three gold medals at the Grenoble Olympics in 1968, is clearly a competitor. From a competitor's standpoint, Killy says what really compels skiers is the sense of personal accomplishment and sheer exhilaration the sport provides. He writes: "From the beginner who has just made his first stem turn to the top racer who has put in a winning run on a slalom course, the feeling of satisfaction and

A SPORT FOR THE BODY AND SOUL

Fridtjof Nansen's book, *Paa Ski Øver Gronland,* recounts the first successful crossing of Greenland on skis. The book served as an introduction to skiing and spurred huge interest in the sport. It not only taught people how to ski, but it taught them why. Nansen, like his fellow Norwegians, embraced skiing as the one sport that benefited both body and mind. Peter Lunn, author of the *Guinness Book of Skiing,* includes an excerpt from Nansen's book.

I know no form of sport which so evenly develops the muscles, which renders the body so strong and elastic, which teaches so well the qualities of dexterity and resources, which in an equal degree calls for decision and resolution. . . . Where will one find more freedom and excitement than when one glides swiftly down the hillside through the trees, one's cheek brushed by the sharp cold air and frosted pine branches, and one's eye, brain and muscles alert and prepared to meet every unknown obstacle and danger which the next instant may throw in one's path? Civilisation is, as it were, washed clean from the mind and left far behind with the city atmosphere and city life; one's whole being is, so to say, wrapped in one's "ski" and the surrounding nature. There is something in the whole which develops soul and not body alone.

achievement is intense, a moment that will long be remembered."[1] For Killy, too, skiing became a way of life.

Skiing is now a way of life for competitors and amateurs alike. A consequence of the sport's popularity is that skiing has become a major tourist industry, generating billions of dollars of income that benefits ski resort operators and, in some cases, entire towns. Ski enthusiasts often travel in order to ski the most popular mountains. For this reason, the population of resort towns swells during ski season. Statistics on the economic impact of the ski industry in the United States are scarce, but regional statistics hint at the incredible popularity of skiing—and the

staggering amount of money the sport generates. According to Dean Lunt, a reporter for the *Portland Press Herald,* the ski industry is an important part of Maine's winter tourism economy. He writes: "A study by Ski Maine, an industry association, pegged economic impact at $250 million per year, including about $100 million at such places as hotels and restaurants."[2] New Hampshire's numbers are even bigger. Ski New Hampshire, an organization that tracks the ski industry, offers statistics for the 1999–2000 season. The organization breaks the figure down into direct sales at the resorts and secondary sales at places such as hotels, restaurants, convenience stores, service stations, retail stores, and even tollbooths. All told, New Hampshire's 2.6 million skiers pumped $566.1 million into the local economy.

Naturally, these impressive figures have caught the attention of corporate executives both here and abroad, and skiing has finally gone commercial. In the United States, a handful of ski resort companies actually appear on the stock exchange, alongside other major corporations. The commercialization of skiing began with smaller resorts being purchased and operated by larger chains. American Skiing Company, for example, owns six resorts in New England and recently expanded to

Skiers crowd an outdoor restaurant at Beaver Creek Mountain in Colorado. Today, skiing is a multimillion-dollar-a-year industry.

THE FIRST AMERICAN SKI RESORT: SUN VALLEY

A railroad tycoon financed the first ski resort in the United States. His inspiration for the idea came directly from the Alps, as John Samuel, author of *The Love of Skiing,* explains.

Americans vacationing in the Alps liked what they saw, but lacking the know-how to transport an Austrian village intact, as they were subsequently to transport London Bridge to Arizona, they brought over the Austrians handy with ski ideas and tools to an Idaho sheep pasture, just north of Kechum. Here, Count Felix Schaffgotsch, an Austrian expert commissioned by W. Averell Harriman, found his ideal—the sun-washed, treeless slopes of Mount Baldy. The Union Pacific Railway, Mr. Harriman's company, wrote the cheque and in 1936–37 Sun Valley gushed, the first purpose-built ski resort in North America.

Sun Valley, Idaho, was America's first ski resort.

Colorado and California. According to Leigh Gallagher of *Forbes Magazine,* the American Skiing Company's 1998 revenue was $317 million, and Vail Resorts, owners of Vail and three other Colorado ski resorts, had revenue of $431.8 million.

Beyond lining the pockets of corporate investors or keeping small towns afloat, skiing brings money to governments both here and abroad. In the United States, for example, the U.S. Forest Service leases some of its land to ski operators. Andrew

Bigford of *Ski* magazine, who estimated the number of skiers in 1999 at 30 million, claims that skiers have a huge economic impact. He says that skiers "give a significant boost to ski town economies from coast to coast, while also generating about $25 million annually in fees for the Forest Service."[3]

Most of the profits generated from skiing come from downhill skiing alone. In contrast to downhill, which requires groomed hills and lift tickets, cross-country skiing is essentially a free sport, one that can be enjoyed on flat, wooded terrain. It is cross-country skiing that the Norwegians practiced and promoted. Surely, Fridtjof Nansen never dreamed that a sport that pushed civilization so far from his mind would become such an integral part of civilization and its economy. The true irony of skiing is that even before the Norwegians used skis as a form of recreation, ancient man used skis as a form of transportation. In prehistoric times, skis were as essential to a hunter's survival as a spear or an arrow. Today, skiing continues to be an essential part of a great number of people's livelihoods. Entire towns thrive on the income generated by skiing's tourist dollars. Some towns, in fact, depend on it. This, of course, is of little concern to the skiers who depend on nothing more than the beauty of the great outdoors, the thrill of racing down a mountainside, and the joy of leaving their cares behind, if only for a day.

CHAPTER 1

The Birth of Skiing: Cross-Country

THE SPORT OF skiing encompasses a variety of forms. In addition to cross-country skiing, there are downhill skiing, ski jumping, and freestyle skiing. Each sport has its own history, but they share a common beginning, for all forms of skiing can be traced back to the origins of cross-country. In fact, the history of skiing began with cross-country skiing (also known as Nordic skiing) thousands of years ago.

The earliest evidence of skiing dates back to 2500 B.C. However, it is difficult to trace the history of skiing because evidence is scarce. Unlike the ancient pieces of pottery or human bones buried in the earth that give archeologists clues to long-lost civilizations, skis deteriorate over time. This is because primitive skis were made of wood—a biodegradable material. In fact, the oldest ski in existence is made of a pine plank and very similar in length and width to a modern ski. It was discovered in 1921 in Hoting, Sweden, and is thought to be forty-five hundred years old. A rock carving in Norway shows a figure on skis that is thought to have been made around the same time as the Hoting ski—2500 B.C. Skiing, therefore, is thought to have originated in these Scandinavian countries, from which it eventually spread to Europe, the United States, and around the globe.

Early Uses of Skis

Although the first skiers may have lived thousands of years ago, ancient skis did

A Norwegian petroglyph from 2500 B.C. depicts a figure on long skis.

not belong to athletes from a bygone era. Instead, they belonged to people who used skis for transportation. Back then, skiing was not even considered a sport. Instead, it was simply a means of survival, a way for hunters in cold climates to move across the snow in search of food. Skiing became an alternative to walking in deep snow. Skis distributed the skier's weight more evenly and, as a result, prevented the skier from sinking into the snow. Thus, the skier could move easily and quickly, which facilitated hunting. Ted Bays, author of *Nine Thousand Years of Skis*, equates skis to other prehistoric tools that enabled early humans to survive. He theorizes: "Many modern skiers live to ski. Ten thousand years ago, they skied to live."[4] Without skis, it is unlikely that any prehistoric human could have lived in cold, inhospitable climates.

For centuries, skiing continued to be used as a practical form of transportation. Just as skis first served as an alternative to walking, they later served as an alternative to riding horses. Before the advent of trains and automobiles, horses were the primary mode of transportation, but they too had trouble getting through deep snow, and they required care such as food and shelter—which was sometimes not practical, especially in remote regions. For example, the military in Norway and Sweden used skis in areas where horses were not practical because of deep snow. There are accounts of skis used in battle in Norway during the country's civil war in 1206. Skis were used in Sweden to defeat the Danes in 1523. They were even used in the United States during World War II by a group of American soldiers known as the Tenth Mountain Division, who were stationed in Italy's Apennine mountain range.

Skis turned out to be more practical than boats for the delivery of certain goods such as mail, too. In the United States, boats were used for transportation up and down the coast or from one coast to the other. Trips were very long because they required an indirect route—traveling around the United States as opposed to across it. It typically took three months for mail to be delivered from New York to San Francisco by boat, for example. Skis offered a more direct route, which made for a faster trip. With the use of skis, mail could be delivered from New York to San Francisco in just twelve days.

The Father of Cross-Country Skiing

Just as skis enabled mail carriers to traverse great distances, they allowed adventurers to explore new lands. It is one adventurer's account of his trek across Greenland that is thought to have inspired people to take up skiing as a recreational sport. In 1890, Fridtjof Nansen of Oslo, Norway, published an account of his journey across southern Greenland on skis. His book is considered by historians to have had a great influence on skiing, which up to the time of his journey was not widely known. His book became a best-seller, and he came to be considered the father of cross-country skiing.

Crossing deep snow on skis, two soldiers carry infant prince Hakon Hakonsson to safety during Norway's civil war in 1206 A.D.

Nansen was an explorer. He was inspired to cross Greenland by newspaper accounts of explorers who had attempted to reach Greenland's interior, a mythical place where the ice was believed to give way to an oasis of green land. Each of these explorers had started their journey from the west coast and, at some point, turned around to head back to where they had started. Nansen decided to begin his journey on the uninhabited east coast, with the goal of finishing the journey on the west coast. He and his crew arrived by boat on August 10 and trudged up the coast on snowshoes before starting their journey on skis on September 2. They skied for nineteen days and covered 248 miles. The journey was a success. Moreover, Nansen attributed his success to skis, claiming that the team of explorers would have had to turn back or would have possibly even perished without the benefit of skis.

Outside of Norway, people knew very little about skis. One German newspaper, in fact, mistakenly reported that Nansen and his party were traveling on skates. Nansen's book introduced the general public to skiing. Moreover, because skiing was such an integral part of the journey, he decided to attribute an entire chapter of the book to skiing, in effect writing the first how-to book on the sport. According to Peter Lunn, author of the *Guinness Book of Skiing*, "he was writing for a public that knew absolutely nothing about skiing

Explorer Fridtjof Nansen is considered to be the father of cross-country skiing.

and he judged it necessary to explain the most basic facts."[5]

The Norwegian Masters

It is assumed that Nansen was a natural on skis because he was a native of Norway, where children grew up skiing. Nicholas Howe, a writer for *Skiing* magazine, says:

NANSEN, THE INVENTOR

Fridtjof Nansen's accomplishments are celebrated in "Hero of the Arctic," written for *Geographical Magazine* by Roland Huntford. As it turns out, Nansen was more than an explorer, he was an inventor. Before becoming an explorer, he was a marine biologist and pioneered a neuron theory, becoming a founder of neurology. As an explorer, he designed a ship to withstand the pressure of ice for polar exploration. As Huntford explains, ingenuity paved the way for Nansen's successful crossing of Greenland.

Nansen introduced skis to polar travel. He also, incidentally, contrived a new kind of sledge with broad, ski-like runners that is still used and which bears his name. He designed an insulated cooking pot, long in use and also called after him, and for good measure he was the first polar explorer to apply the layer principle to clothing, and the first to calculate diet analytically—in the dawn of scientific nutrition, as it happened. Thus he laid the foundations of modern polar technique. He also opened what is called the heroic age of polar exploration—the fight to be first at the North and South poles before the advent of mechanical transport. But it was

Fridtjof Nansen's inventions initiated the sport of skiing.

Nansen's use of skis that had the most far-reaching consequences. The first crossing of Greenland launched skiing as a universal sport.

"Norwegian boys learn jumping and cross-country as fish learn swimming."[6] As a result, many Norwegians became masters of ski techniques. While it is not clear exactly where and when skiing evolved from a practical form of transportation into a favorite pastime in Norway, historians point to the publication of Nansen's book as the beginning of the recreational skiing era. After its publication, wealthy men in Europe suddenly wanted to travel long distances on skis for sport, rather than for necessity. Cross-country ski clubs began to pop up throughout Europe and to recruit experienced Norwegian cross-country skiers as instructors.

Well before the publication of Nansen's book, however, Norwegian masters of skiing had begun immigrating to other regions in search of work, primarily farming. Many of the Norwegian immigrants ended up founding ski clubs in their new homelands. Records indicate that immigrants began to form ski clubs in the United States in the late 1800s, for example. Ski clubs in places such as Minneapolis and Wisconsin had

Norwegian names, and the ski club business was conducted in Norwegian. Some clubs, in fact, restricted their membership to males of Scandinavian origin. For example, the constitution of the Skiklubben club of Berlin, New Hampshire, specifically stated that membership was open to any Scandinavian of good reputation. However, by the turn of the century, the clubs became more Americanized. Clubs welcomed men of all nationalities and conducted their business in English.

THE DARTMOUTH OUTING CLUB

In praising the formation of the first college ski club at Dartmouth, *The Skisport,* a magazine devoted to skiing, took an opportunity to praise the virtues of skiing. These are the virtues that are associated with the Norwegians' philosophy of *idraet*. E. John B. Allen includes an excerpt from the magazine in his book, *From Skisport to Skiing.*

If you love the great out-of-doors, and if you like to live, really live, in the clean, wide distant sweep of a limitless horizon, breathe an untainted air, boundless as the heavens themselves and enjoy a freedom that can be found in no other way, a keen, stimulating, exhilarating pleasure that thrills you through the very center of your being, you will understand what motives led to the organization of the Dartmouth Outing Club.

Members of the first Dartmouth Outing Club race downhill.

The Notion of Idraet

While clubs may have become more Americanized, the attitude toward skiing was purely Norwegian. The Norwegians have a special word for skiing: *idraet.* The American translation of *idraet* is "sport," but it really means something much more specific. *Idraet* specifically refers to outdoor physical exercise. Furthermore, the goal of this particular form of outdoor exercise is the development of strength, manliness, and toughness. At first, *idraet* was believed to perfect the individual: It benefited both the mind and the soul. But, when Norway emerged from Swedish rule in 1905, the Norwegians further embraced *idraet* as a means of rebuilding their nation. So, over time, *idraet* became more than a word. It became an ideal, much like Americans think of the word *patriotism.* According to E. John B. Allen, author of *From Skisport to Skiing,* one Norwegian immigrant who helped found the National Ski Association (NSA) in 1905 in Ishpeming, Michigan, referred to skiing in the NSA's newsletter as the continuation of "their glorious work for the betterment of humanity."[7]

American colleges appear to have been among the first to embrace the spirit of *idraet,* particularly the idea that skiing promotes physical—as well as mental—fitness. Dartmouth College first founded a ski club—known at the time as an outing club—in 1909. Their outings were simply an afternoon of cross-country skiing in the local woods. An article in *National Geographic* featured one of the college's outings. It underscored the idea that skiing benefited the body as well as the mind. The article said: "Not only has the Outing Club improved the physical well being of Dartmouth's student body, but faculty statistics show that scholarship has profited by the weekend excursions of skiing parties."[8]

The members of the Dartmouth Outing Club were fortunate. Dartmouth was situated in a rural area, and club members had easy access to woods and open spaces for cross-country skiing. Soon, this form of outdoor recreation spread beyond the rural colleges and ski clubs to the general public. In the early 1930s, when railroad transportation made travel more affordable, many city dwellers began to travel to the countryside, where they could ski for free in wide-open spaces: They skied on pastures, logging roads, and natural hillocks. The numbers of skiers dramatically increased. By 1934, according to author Morten Lund, "trains were pulling out of New York, Boston, Chicago, San Francisco, Ottawa and Montreal carrying thousands."[9] Thus, a transition in the recreational skiing had begun, and skiing was no longer limited to small clubs.

Equipment Basics

While the notion of *idraet* drew many people to cross-country skiing, another reason it became popular was affordability.

Cross-country skiing requires open land, and the equipment is relatively simple. The first piece of equipment is the ski, the basic design of which has changed little from skiing's earliest history. Early skis were made of long strips of wood. Skis curve up slightly at the front tip. They break through the snow like the bow of a ship breaks through the waves. Skis generally range from three to four inches in width and six to seven feet in length. Later, as downhill skiing became popular, ski manufacturers began to experiment with metal and synthetic materials such as plastic and fiberglass to increase speed, provide more flexibility, and prevent warping or breaking.

Early cross-country skiers used footwear that was similar to everyday footwear. In fact, it is likely that some early skiers simply found a way to attach their everyday footwear to a homemade pair of skis; however, little information about early ski footwear exists. Still, hints about early footwear can be gathered from Alpine skiers, who started the sport of downhill skiing with equipment designed for cross-country skiing. For example, early downhill ski boots were made of leather and looked much like the lace-up boots that gentlemen wore everyday. Over the years, footwear became more specialized. Today, cross-country footwear is light and bendable and resembles a running shoe, usually with nylon or leather uppers. At the toe of the shoe is a metal part that clips into another metal part on the ski, known as the binding. The shoe attaches only at the toe, leaving the heel free to move.

Early poles were made of bamboo and snapped easily. Accounts of races from the 1860s, such as Norway's famed Christiania, which first took place in 1866, describe racers competing with just one pole. The use of two poles did not become popular until twenty years later. According to Peter Lunn, Ernst Bjerknaes of Finland was the first racer to use two poles in an 1887 competition. Lunn writes: "[T]he Finns discovered that two poles were an advantage for cross-country skiing."[10] The reason is that poles helped the skier to balance and to negotiate turns. Poles are stuck (or planted) into the ground during turns. Beginners often use them just to balance, as with a cane or a crutch. Like a crutch, the height of the ski pole should reach the skier's armpit. There are two types of grips for ski poles. Some ski poles are equipped with a handle resembling that of a sword. Others have a plastic or leather strap that wraps around the skier's wrist. Two to three inches above the tip of the pole is something that looks like an upside-down drain cover. This is known as the basket, and it helps to provide a firm hold in the snow. Aluminum poles were invented in 1958 and were more durable than wood poles.

Wax is a critical component of ski equipment for cross-country. Yet, little information exists about how the use of wax came about. It is an idea that was probably tested by various Norwegians in different locations under a variety of circumstances. Regardless of where or when the use of wax began, it grew to become a mainstay of the sport. Wax provides grip and speed. Just as the cross-country boot resembles a running shoe, the cross-country technique resembles a jogger's stride. Wax helps the skis to glide along the snow. Some skis are permanently waxed, and some need to be waxed periodically.

Over the years, the use of wax has evolved into somewhat of a science. Selecting a wax is complicated. The choice primarily depends on snow conditions and the fact that the conditions may change while the skier is en route. Cross-country skiers usually carry wax with them in order to be prepared for changes in conditions. According to the 2002 NBC Olympics website: "Glide wax is used to decrease the friction between the skis and the snow. Kick wax is used to increase friction between the skis and the snow in order to prevent slipping."[11] Glide wax is applied to the front and back tips of the skis, and kick wax is used in the middle.

Technique

Many books are devoted to teaching the traditional technique of cross-country skiing, known as the classical stride technique. Yet, little information exists about the evolution of the cross-country technique. For this reason, it can be assumed that little has changed when it comes to the classical stride. The classical stride can be equated to running, except that the foot never really leaves the ground. Instead, the skier slides each foot forward. Hence, the ski slides forward, making a track in the snow. In the classical stride, each ski follows its own track. The skier's arms move alternately as well, as in running, except that the skier is carrying poles. With this technique, poles are armpit height and are used to push off. The skier swings his or her arm up to shoulder height, plants the pole, and pushes. This provides part of the forward momentum. The major part of the momentum comes from the kick. John Samuel, author of *The Love of Skiing,* explains: "[O]ne arm plants the pole and the opposite leg pushes down and back in a horse-kicking motion, providing the push for the other leg to glide forward."[12] Wax, which helps the ski glide forward, also helps the ski "stick" after the glide, giving the skier some leverage from which to kick forward again. Going downhill, the skier pushes with both poles simultaneously.

The skating step technique (now known as freestyle) is a newer, more controversial way to cross-country ski. It was introduced to the Olympics in 1988. With the skating step, the skier keeps one ski in a

Skiing the freestyle skating technique to perfection, Russia's Mikhail Ivanov crosses the finish line at the 2002 Salt Lake City Winter Olympics.

track and uses the other to push off, as in skating. Glide wax is applied to the entire underside of the skis. The poles used in the skating step are taller than those used in the classical stride, reaching the skier's chin or mouth, presumably because they are used for pushing the skier along rather than just for balance. And while footwear for the classical technique resembles a running shoe, footwear for the skating technique resembles an ice skate. Footwear has more ankle support in the skating technique—again to aid the push.

Cross-country skiers generally follow a relatively straight course, one that involves little turning. However, there are a variety of turning methods used by cross-country skiers. One that is unique to cross-county is like ice skating: pushing off and then bringing the skis together. Two others are used primarily in downhill skiing, but may have originated as cross-country techniques. The first is the stem turn, with the skis in a V point and the skier's weight transferred, forcing the skis and the body to turn. The second is the Telemark turn, a wide turn that involves bending one knee.

Origins of Cross-Country Racing

From its origins as a practical means of transportation, cross-country skiing evolved into a popular form of recreation and a competitive sport. However, the point at which it officially emerged as a sport is unclear. It is difficult to trace the origins of cross-country skiing as a competitive sport, because all early forms of competitive skiing—cross-country, downhill, and ski jumping—share the same beginnings. Early competitions included elements of all three styles, which at the time were all referred to as cross-country. For example, the first records of cross-country ski competitions date back to the Norwegian military, probably in 1767, according to E. John B. Allen. However, these early competitions seem to have focused more on ski jumping and downhill racing as opposed to what is popularly thought of as cross-country racing. Some historians point to the Christiania as the true beginning of competitive cross-country racing.

The first Christiania was held in Oslo (Oslo was formerly known as Christiania) in Norway in 1866 and featured cross-country skiing and ski jumping as a combined event (in 1883, the events were separated, but competitors continued to compete in both).

The Winter Olympics were first conceived as a showcase for cross-country competition. Winter sports were featured in the Olympics as early as 1908, when the British Olympic Council sponsored exhibition figure skating events for women and men. In 1920, when the Summer Games resumed after World War I, both figure skating and men's ice hockey appeared as exhibition sports. The Norwegian Skiing Federation put pressure on the International Olympic Committee (IOC) to designate a separate Winter Games for cross-country and ski jumping. That pressure, combined with the popularity of the newly invented downhill and slalom skiing in the 1920s, convinced the IOC to establish the Olympic Winter Games. The first international World Championship in 1924 in Chamonix, France, was retroactively designated as the first Winter Olympic Games in 1925, and the Chamonix winners are listed in the Olympic records as the first Winter Olympic medalists. The focus of the World Championship—now known as the first official Winter Olympics—was strictly cross-country (downhill events were banned). According to Lund: "At the beginning of the 1920s, jumping and cross-country racing were the only games in town in terms of officially recognized international ski competition."[13]

In cross-country, competitors race against each other—and the clock—with the winner being the first to cross the finish line, which means completing the course in the least amount of time. The first Winter Olympics featured a 15-kilometer and a 50-kilometer classical for men only. Over the years, more events were added, and the freestyle technique was introduced. Otherwise, the sport has remained much the same.

Women's cross-country events were added in 1952, beginning with a 10-kilometer classical. In fact, it was not until around 1950 that women were first taken seriously in the sport of skiing. According to E. John B. Allen, "Before World War II, women participated only peripherally in Nordic ski competition."[14] He says that was because women's bodies were thought to be unable to withstand a race over distance. Jumping, he says, was simply out of the question.

In today's Winter Olympics, cross-country consists of twelve events, the primary focus of which is strength and endurance. Speed counts, however, because the first to cross the finish line is the winner. The sprint features a series of elimination rounds. All other races feature a mass start. There are separate events for

men and women, the main difference being that the distance for the men's events is longer than for the women's. First, there is a classical (10 kilometers and 30 kilometers for women and 15 kilometers and 50 kilometers for men), which features the traditional straight-striding technique in tracks. Then there is a freestyle (15 kilometers for women and 30 kilometers for men), which features the skating technique. Next, there is a sprint (1.5 kilometers for men and women), in which racers use either the classical or the freestyle stride. There is also a combined pursuit for both men and women. This involves two separate races. The first is a 5-kilometer classical, and the second is a 5-kilometer freestyle. Finally, there is a relay (4 x 5-kilometer relay for women and 4 x 10-kilometer relay for men). Each team is composed of four skiers, each of whom skis one of the four 5-kilometer or 10-kilometer relay legs. The first two legs of the relay are classical style. The final two are freestyle.

While cross-country skiing may have originated in Norway, the Norwegians have faced some tough competition from other countries for Olympic medals. The Soviet Union, in particular, has produced some outstanding cross-country athletes. Throughout its Olympic history, the most cross-country medals have been won by athletes from the Soviet Union, followed closely by Norway. The Soviets have a total of seventy-seven medals (twenty-eight of which are gold) and the Norwegians have a total of seventy-three.

The Governing Body of Competitive Skiing

The IOC governs the Winter Olympics. However, an International Ski Federation (ISF) makes the rules for ski races, determines eligibility, approves courses for international competition, sanctions events eligible for ISF points (a complicated formula based on race results from a series of events that determines a competitive skier's international standing), and approves the courses for Olympic competition. The ISF was established in 1924, about one week after the first Winter Olympic Games had been held. It is officially known as Federation Internationale de Ski (FIS), but is commonly referred to in the United States as the International Ski Federation, or ISF. Prior to the formation of the ISF, an organization known as the International Ski Congress was skiing's main governing body. It was established in 1910 to govern the numerous ski clubs that had become popular at the beginning of the twentieth century.

At the time the ISF was established, it represented fourteen countries and focused primarily on cross-country. Today,

Women push off at the start of the fifteen-kilometer freestyle cross-country race at the 2002 Winter Olympics.

THE BIATHLON

The biathlon, an event that combines distance skiing with marksmanship, is often considered part of the cross-country tradition. Kim Clark of *U.S. News & World Report* says the sport started out as a friendly rivalry between Norwegian and Swedish border guards, who would race on their cross-country skis and stop to shoot rifles at targets. The sport is popular in Europe, where races attract huge crowds, but it has yet to catch on in the United States. Clark provides basic race strategies in her article entitled "Biathlon: Grab Your Rifles and Head for a Scandinavian Snow-down."

Americans who tune in [to the 2002 Olympics] may find that the biathlon can be exciting. In the relays, the skiers race up and down the countryside, then glide into a firing range, pull .22-caliber rifles from their backs, and fire at targets, before skiing back to tag a teammate. Jeremy Teela, one of the U.S. team's few medal prospects, says there's lots of hidden strategy. If he has skied too fast, for example, his leg muscles twitch, throwing off his aim. That can be a race-losing mistake, as one missed target means a 150–meter [164 yard] penalty loop. Rachel Steer, who like Teela grew up in Alaska, says there are technological secrets, too. Each skier brings about 10 pairs of skis, designed for different kinds of snow. And the team has dedicated "wax technician" who figures out which wax will speed them along best.

Germany's Uschi Disl (number 37) leads the 2002 Olympic biathlon.

it represents forty-eight countries and focuses on downhill, freestyle, jumping, and snowboarding, in addition to cross-country—all of which have become Olympic events. At the same time that the Winter Olympic Games were conceived, the newly formed ISF also proposed a World Ski Championship. This event was known until 1927 as the "rendez-vous" and was later called the FIS Competitions. Today, it is known as the World Championship. In addition to the Winter Olympics and the World Championship, there is a World Cup of ski racing. The World Cup takes place every year, the World Championship takes place every two years, and the Winter Olympics take place every four years.

Cross-country skiing has evolved from its prehistoric beginnings as a means of survival. Surely no hunter skiing through the wilderness in search of prey ever dreamed that cross-country skiing would reach such popularity and that the activity would become an Olympic sport. Thanks to an early human's idea of fashioning a pair of primitive skis from a pine log, millions of people now enjoy what Fridtjof Nansen best described as the "freedom and the excitement" of gliding "swiftly down the hillside through the trees."[15]

CHAPTER 2

The Downhill Craze

DOWNHILL SKIING IS vastly different from cross-country skiing, but both styles of skiing originated in response to the terrain. Cross-country skiing is a means of traveling over relatively flat terrain. Downhill skiing—as the name implies—is a means of traveling down hills—often, very steep, treacherous hills. The transition from cross-country to downhill began with a few adventurous souls, but downhill soon became one of the world's most popular recreational sports. Innovations in ski techniques, ski equipment, and ski instruction allowed the average person to take up a sport that had previously been reserved for those who were athletic and those who were affluent.

Early History

Downhill skiing is also known as Alpine skiing. The name comes from a region in Europe with steep mountains known as the Alps. The European Alps can be found in Germany, Austria, Switzerland, Italy, and France, which today are home to many of the world's most popular ski resorts. Alpine skiing began in those regions around the late 1800s. As in the history of cross-country skiing, it is difficult to piece together the early history of downhill skiing. This is primarily because skiing is an individualized sport, and skiers who first learned how to maneuver their skis on inclines were mostly self-taught. These early skiers included Norwegians, who had encountered occasional inclines in their cross-country treks or who sought out inclines in a quest to learn to jump (ski jumping began as part of the cross-country tradition). It is also possible that some Norwegians immigrated to the Alps, where skiing downhill presented a new, personal challenge. Early skiers also included people from the Alps who had adopted cross-country techniques and were in the process of adapting them to their region.

Historians generally agree that the invention of turning techniques marked the turning point from Nordic (cross-country) to Alpine (downhill). The first widely known turning technique was the Telemark turn. Telemark is a plateau fifty miles southwest of what is now Oslo, the capital of Norway. It was home to mountain farmers, who were the first to control the speed of their skis with a turning motion that relied on the skis themselves, rather than on poles. The Telemark turn is a swooping motion in which skiers crouch, bending their inside leg (in a kneeling

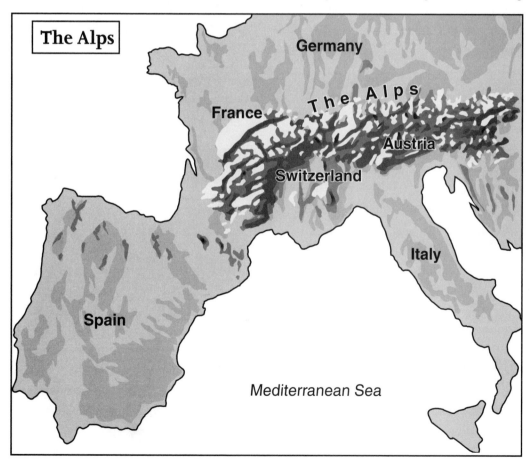

The Alps

Germany

France

The Alps

Austria

Switzerland

Italy

Spain

Mediterranean Sea

position with the heel raised) and shifting their weight to the outside. The crouched position helps to lower their center of gravity and provides stability through the turn. The turn may have originated as a means of stopping after a jump, but it also provided a means of controlling speed in general. Of the famed Telemark athletes, one name stands out: Sondre Norheim.

Sondre Norheim

Sondre Norheim popularized the Telemark turn, although it is not clear if he alone invented it. It was during the 1868 Christiania that he demonstrated the turn, which had never before been seen by many of the spectators in the crowd. The Christiania, held annually since 1866 and known as the first official competition in ski history, featured cross-country and ski jumping as a combined event. There, the Telemark turn was featured as a way to stop after jumping. Like champion athletes of today, Norheim made the new technique look effortless. The crowd marveled at his style and grace, and Norheim became known as the father of ski jumping.

It seems that the Telemark turn, however, was limited to people of athletic ability such as Norheim. In the early days of downhill, other skiers preferred to rely on poles—or sticks, as they called them—to brake and to control their speed. Braking with this method was awkward. It required that skiers dig their sticks into the ground,

Sondre Norheim introduced the Telemark turn at the 1868 Christiania.

which was a difficult task because the skier needed to put a lot of weight on the pole. The best way to put weight on a stick was to ride it. Stickriding was the technique of choice in the late 1880s and early 1890s. Peter Lunn, author of the *Guinness Book of Skiing*, says: "[stickriders] sat astride their pole, like a witch on her broomstick, so that their weight on the pole exerted a braking effect."[16] Another method was not to ride the stick, but simply to lean back on it in order to brake.

In the case of stickriding and the Telemark turn, it appears that early downhill skiing was limited to those who were daring and athletic, and it seems that the primary motivations for downhill skiing were fun and adventure. Yet, for downhill skiing to become a popular recreational activity, an easier method of controlling speed was needed. It was the invention of the stem turn that eventually allowed people of average athletic ability to take up downhill skiing. Lund says it made "skiing in a slow, controlled manner a possibility for beginners—a fine introduction to skiing for a city-bound clientele with limited practice time."[17]

The Stem Turn

The stem turn was invented in the 1890s by Mathias Zdarsky of Austria, who was inspired to take up skiing after reading Fridtjof Nansen's tale of skiing across Greenland. Zdarsky practiced at Lilienfeld (sixty miles southwest of Vienna), using traditional cross-country skis. Like Norheim, he invented his own way of traveling downhill with controlled speed. What he discovered is that a downhill skier needs to turn frequently, using broad zigzags to make his way down the slope. The turn is accomplished by angling the skis in a V (turning them into a plow) and using the edges of the skis to dig into the slope to keep from slipping. Zdarsky also invented his own heel binding for this purpose, although it is not clear what the binding looked like. Of Zdarsky's turn, Samuel writes: "It dominated Alpine technical thinking for the next 70 years, and elements remain in the most modern techniques."[18]

Nansen's adventure story not only inspired Zdarsky to take up skiing, it inspired him to publish a book. While Nansen's book focused primarily on his adventure, Zdarsky's book was strictly about technique. And, just as Nansen's book is credited with launching a cross-country craze, Zdarsky's book is credited with launching a downhill craze. Suddenly,

Mathias Zdarsky, father of Alpine skiing, skis downhill with a large pole used for balance on turns.

people flocked to Lilienfeld to learn Zdarsky's technique in the free classes he offered. Zdarsky became known as the father of downhill skiing and is credited with opening the first downhill ski school—an idea that would be perfected by a fellow Austrian.

Johann "Hannes" Schneider

As downhill gained popularity, hotels began to operate ski schools in order to attract clientele, especially during the winter months. Wealthy individuals were already in the habit of vacationing in the Alps, where they enjoyed hiking as well as fine restaurants and posh accommodations. So, Alpine skiing began as a way to extend the tourist season. Morten Lund, author of "A Short History of Alpine Skiing," says: "Alpine skiing was an elite venture practiced by a few hardy souls in a half dozen mountain resorts in the European Alps—where, inns and hotels had just begun to stay open in winter."[19]

Ski resorts in the Austrian Alps operate downhill ski schools.

The key to attracting a larger clientele was to make skiing easy for people of average athletic ability. At Austrian hotels, for example, local ski guides provided instruction, usually by demonstrating their personal method rather than adhering to any particular standard. Johann Schneider, who had mastered both the Telemark and stem turn techniques at an early age, was working as a ski guide for a hotel at the age of sixteen in 1906. He would go on to standardize ski instruction and play an integral role in downhill's history.

Schneider became a ski instructor during World War I. The experience of teaching thousands of soldiers how to ski is what led him to open his own highly successful ski school. His method of teaching became the standard. According to Lund, "The Schneider system replaced the tradition of ski guides, each teaching his own grab-bag of turns and operating from scattered hotels throughout the town."[20]

THE TENTH MOUNTAIN DIVISION

Hannes Schneider, founder of the Arlberg school of ski instruction, developed his famous technique while instructing ski troops in Austria during World War I. After the war, Arlberg's troops fanned out to ski schools and helped to popularize downhill skiing. Ski troops were not used in the United States until World War II. According to Morten Lund, author of "A Short History of Alpine Skiing," the First Battalion, Eighty-seventh Infantry, was activated in June 1941. They went on to train at Camp Hale in Colorado as the Tenth Mountain Division. There, soldiers were instructed in the Arlberg method.

The common bond of skiing built the Tenth into a formidable outfit which was undeterred by one of the war's heaviest casualty rates among American divisions: thirty percent of its men were killed or wounded in the 10th Division-led breakthrough from Italy's Apennines to the Brenner Pass in 1945. After the war, several thousand 10th Mountain survivors, Army-minted Arlbergers, went into skiing—a vigorous cadres of inventors, developers, teachers and entrepreneurs. Friedle Pfeifer founded the ski resort at Aspen and later Peter Seibert founded its closest rival, Vail, the two giant resorts of the era. In all, some 62 resorts were either founded by, directed by or had ski schools run by 10th Mountain veterans; two thousand of them had gone into the ranks of ski instructors.

Schneider standardized skiing by creating a sequence of classes, which became known as the Arlberg system—named after his birthplace. Each class was geared to a particular level of ability. Beginning skiers progressed from one level to the next, until they became proficient at skiing. Schneider also developed a logical sequence for teaching turns, beginning with the stem turn and progressing to more difficult turns. The teaching method involved strict ethics and a disciplined approach—ideas he adapted from his military experience.

Skiing for the Masses

After World War I, when Schneider founded his ski school in Saint Anton, Austria, traveling to remote locations was expensive. One reason that Schneider chose Saint Anton as his base of operation was its proximity to the Orient Express, which supplied him with wealthy travelers from London, Munich, Vienna, and Berlin. However, as the development of cars, trains, and airplanes provided more people with a means of affordable transportation, the number of skiers steadily increased. By the 1930s in the United States, for example, Lund says trains went everywhere. He writes: "Being a skier required only roundtrip fare . . . warm clothes and rental equipment—all affordable even by a clerical worker."[21]

Schneider had also trained other instructors to teach the Arlberg method. In that way, beginners could pick up lessons where they left off, as long as they located an Arlberg instructor. Schneider attracted top instructors, some of whom competed in downhill races. Lund says: "By the end of the school's first decade, Schneider's school had a half dozen of the best alpine racers in the world on its teaching staff."[22]

By the 1930s, Austrian ski instructors—including numerous Arlberg instructors—had fanned out around the globe. The first Arlberg instructor to teach in the United States was headquartered at Peckett's Inn in Sugar Hill, New Hampshire. The invasion of Austria in 1938 by Nazi Germany prompted many more Austrians to immigrate to the United States. (In fact, the Nazis imprisoned Schneider, but he was freed in 1939 and immigrated to the United States, where he taught at Mount Cranmore in New Hampshire.) The Austrians—and Schneider, in particular—are credited with popularizing downhill skiing in the United States and beyond.

Another reason for an increase in skiers was the new medium of film. Schneider collaborated with a filmmaker to produce the world's first ski film in 1920. Schneider himself became the star of subsequent films produced by the same filmmaker, becoming the world's first action hero (billed on the big screen as "Hannes" instead of "Johann"), according to Lund. His last film was released in 1930, and by then the Arlberg technique had become the worldwide standard.

Downhill Equipment

While the invention of new ski techniques ushered in the downhill craze, it was the invention of new ski equipment that helped the average person to master the new techniques. Just as downhill techniques were adapted from existing cross-country techniques, downhill ski equipment was adapted from cross-country equipment. The first major adaptation was the addition of a rear binding.

Sondre Norheim invented the first heel binding in 1850. Because downhill skiing began as part of the cross-country tradition, the same equipment was used for both. Early changes in ski equipment were usually the result of a skier adapting the existing equipment to better suit a certain purpose, such as jumping or turning, as was the case with Norheim. Cross-country skis were traditionally attached to the skier's footwear at the toe, using a clip. The cross-country skier glided his skis forward in a way that resembled jogging, in which the heel was constantly raised and lowered. This was a fine arrangement for moving in a straight line. It became a problem for turning because the heel could slip off the ski when trying to angle the ski for a turn. Anchoring the heel to the ski gave the skier more control, and it made turning much easier.

Norheim's invention featured a leather strap that acted like a belt. It ran from one side of the ski, up and over the boot, and to the other side of the ski. The invention allowed him to perfect his now famous Telemark turn.

While Norheim's binding was designed with skiing in mind, other bindings were designed with safety in mind. As skiing gained popularity in the 1930s, more accidents occurred. In particular, people who only skied occasionally—such as weekend

Johann Schneider performs a Telemark turn.

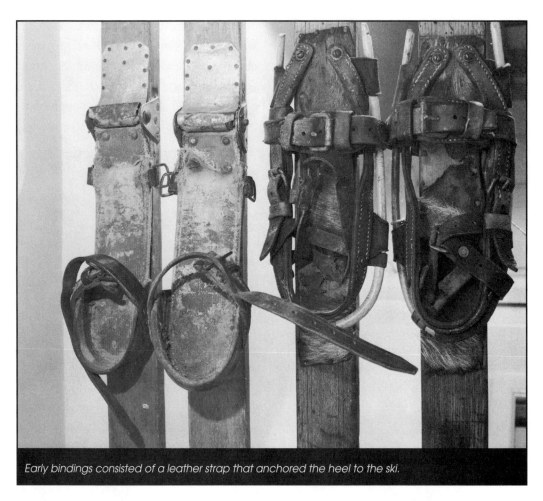

Early bindings consisted of a leather strap that anchored the heel to the ski.

or vacation skiers—seemed to be at risk of dangerous falls. It was during this time in Great Britain that the safety binding was introduced. Samuel writes that it was "a simple strap pulling the heel cable off the boot in a forward fall. As time went on bindings became much more sophisticated, providing for sideways, forward and backward release."[23] The invention resulted in fewer broken legs and strained ligaments.

In Alpine skiing today, there are two types of bindings: heel and toe bindings and plate bindings. With heel and toe bindings, the boot is equipped with a clip in the toe that fastens to the ski. Bindings are located on the back of the boot and serve a dual purpose. They keep the boot (and the skier) attached to the ski. At the same time, they allow the boot to release from the ski when the skier falls. This is a key to reducing injury. A skier who falls will more than likely take a few tumbles down the incline of the hill. This is especially true for skiers at high speeds. If the ski is not released, it will force the foot and leg to twist, causing strains, fractures, and painful breaks. Just as a ski must be suited to a particular skier, so too must the binding. It has to be adjusted for weight, height, and ability.

Plate bindings work the same way as heel and toe bindings, but use a different design. With plate bindings, the entire boot is attached to a metal plate, which is attached to the ski. In a fall, the plate detaches. The benefit of plate bindings is that they are easier to remount.

When a skier falls and the skis detach, there is the possibility that the skis will continue to slide down the slope. Not only is it difficult for a skier to walk down a slope to retrieve a ski, but the runaway ski might hit and possibly injure another skier. To prevent this, skis can be equipped with prongs that dig into the snow upon being detached. Or, they can be equipped with a safety strap that the skier ties around his or her ankle. However, the safety strap presents its own dangers, especially at high speeds when a strapped ski can begin to turn—or windmill—in the air and hit the skier. The prongs—dubbed ski brakes—

Today, skiers wear modern heel and toe ski bindings that easily release if the skier falls.

EARLY SKI POLES

In 1867, a ski competition was held in Oslo, Norway. Known as the Christiania, this event eventually evolved into one of the most prestigious competitions in the world. In the *Guinness Book of Skiing,* Peter Lunn describes an anonymous author's account of early ski poles and how they were used in the very first competition.

A contemporary account describes how competitors of this period relied on their single long, thick pole, not only to reduce speed, but also for support, leaning their weight right back against the pole dragging in the snow. [The author] also describes how frightened competitors looked as they approached the jump, how frantically they tried to reduce speed with the pole, and how they did not try to leap, but simply plopped over the jump, covering a bare 4 to 5m (13–16ft).

became the industry standard in 1975, replacing the safety strap.

The Shape of the Ski

Another equipment contribution Norheim made to downhill skiing is a change in the design of the ski itself. Norheim was the first to change the shape of the ski to better suit jumping and turning in the 1860s. His ski design was shorter and narrower than skis that were used at the time. His ski was 1.9 meters long, which was two feet shorter than skis that were used at the time, and 2.7 inches wide, compared to the standard ski of the time, which was 3.3 inches at the front and 2.9 inches at the tail. These new dimensions made skis easier to control in downhill skiing and became the industry standard that is still used today.

The first major innovation in ski material was laminating, which began in Norway in the late 1800s but did not become popular until the 1930s and 1940s. Instead of using a single wood board, manufacturers began layering two or three thinner pieces of wood together with glue. This layered effect provided greater flexibility, which prevented warping and breaking. By the 1950s, almost all downhill skis were laminated.

Manufacturers also had begun experimenting with new materials for skis, with first metal, then plastic, then fiberglass becoming popular choices. Metal-edged skis—which provided better turning and, thus, more control—were first introduced in 1928 and popularized by Rudolph Lettner. Howard Head of Baltimore developed the first mass-produced metal ski in 1947, which were nicknamed "cheaters" because turning on Head skis was so much easier than turning on wooden ones. Samuel writes: "By the ease with which they turned on it, hundreds of thousands of semi-fit city dwellers could tackle the red runs [more advanced runs] previously denied them."[24]

The first all-plastic ski was introduced in 1954, followed by fiberglass skis, which became the industry standard in the 1960s. Samuel says that ski manufacturing reached a level of sophistication by the mid-1970s that allowed all major manufacturers to produce skis that were both strong and flexible, and that "this was the great leap forward."[25]

In addition to innovations in ski materials, boots were constantly being improved—all for the purposes of increasing comfort

THE HEAD STANDARD

The Head Standard was a revolutionary metal ski. Prior to the Head Standard, which was introduced in 1949, skis were made out of wood. John Samuel, author of *The Love of Skiing*, says the new design changed ski construction for all time.

> It had an aluminum top and bottom, plastic sides, and a core of sandwiched plywood layers set on edge. It was an American production-line job which did not have to be hand-made. It required no special care, it did not warp, and broke only under extreme stress. It was three times as flexible at the tips as a wooden ski, and turned easily in soft snow.

and control. The boot is an important piece of ski equipment because the boot is what dictates the skier's level of comfort. Whereas cross-country skiing requires lighter, more flexible boots, downhill skiing requires rigid boots—hence, comfort is a challenge. Back in the days when skis were made of wood, boots were made of leather. Leather is a pliable material, which can conform to the shape of the foot. This made leather boots comfortable. However, some skiers complained that the boots became stretched out, just as an old, well-worn shoe. Moreover, leather boots were laced up and did not provide the support needed for precise maneuvering. The first buckle boot was introduced in 1955, and the first plastic boot with buckles was introduced in 1957. Lund says: "[B]uckles in combination with plastic provided the close fit that gave skiers the precise control over the skis taken for granted today."[26] With plastic, the foot must adjust to the shape of the boot (as opposed to leather, which adapts to the shape of the foot). Some boots are equipped with an inner liner that molds to the shape of the foot, increasing comfort. With the addition of buckles and dials, new, more advanced designs allow the boot itself to be adjusted to the shape of the foot and give the skier the ability to loosen or tighten various sections of the boot.

UNIFORMS

Ski attire has always been an important part of ski equipment. A look at the history of ski attire reveals that uniforms were once the standard. Members of ski clubs formed by Norwegians who immigrated to the United States in the late 1800s wore uniforms that were reminiscent of the military. E. John B. Allen, author of *From Skisport to Skiing,* writes about the attention paid to proper dress in the sport of skiing.

Discussions of outfits occurred almost immediately after a club was founded. Ishpeming [one early club founder] came out in favor of tight fitting suits in November 1901. In December, caps and leggings were discussed, and the "long-wished for suits" were first used in a parade in March. Colors were also important. Aurora's; "red cap, white blouse, blue knee breeches, red stockings and blue belt" reflected the red, white, and blue of the old and new homelands [referring to Norway and the United States]. Clubs gained social cohesion as well as exclusiveness by wearing uniforms.

Skiing Is Now a Big Business

It was with these innovations in technique, equipment, and instruction that the average individual became a weekend skier. Today, resorts around the globe cater to weekend skiers. As Lund noted, downhill skiing began with just a few people and mountain resorts in the European Alps. Today, it is estimated that 20 million skiers visit the Alps each year. This figure represents locals (12 million people live in the Alps) who enjoy skiing in the area and tourists who are drawn to the Alps because of its reputation for great skiing.

The sport of skiing continues to be most closely associated with the places it originated, such as Norway and Austria, but skiing now abounds in Canada, the United States, and such far-flung regions as Argentina, Turkey, Siberia, Scotland, and Japan. Ski enthusiasts can traverse the globe in search of new trails and new challenges. Die-hard skiers are no longer confined to a single season, as they once were in the Alps. When the ski season ends in New England, for example, devoted skiers cross the equator to ski in Australia and New Zealand, where the ski season (June through October) is opposite that of the United States. Lund writes: "[A]lpine skiing has reached a popularity and a global penetration far beyond the wildest dreams of its pioneers."[27]

CHAPTER 3

The Age of Downhill Racing

 E ARLY CROSS-COUNTRY RACES involved elements of both downhill racing and ski jumping. Over time, these became more specialized and were contested as individual sports. While the history of downhill racing got its start in the 1700s with cross-country skiing, it did not emerge as its own sport until the early 1900s. Although downhill racing was popular from the beginning, it was another three decades before it was officially recognized as a sport and added to the Olympic roster of events.

Early Downhill Races

Historians generally point to Switzerland as the official starting place of downhill racing, but they differ on the exact date and location of its origin. Downhill racing

began in much the same way as downhill recreational skiing: It was envisioned as a way to extend the tourist season in the Alps—primarily as a form of amusement, a way for amateurs to test their ability on the slopes in a competitive setting. It is Arnold Lunn of Great Britain who is credited with inventing downhill and slalom racing by historians such as E. John B. Allen, author of *From Skisport to Skiing*. Yet, other historians such as John Samuel point to Arnold's father, Henry, as the one who initiated the idea.

According to Samuel, Henry was a travel agent of sorts, although the profession did not officially exist back then. In the 1890s, he founded the Public Schools Alpine Sports Club and arranged Alpine ski vacation packages to Swiss ski centers such as Adelboden, Klosters, Montana, Wengen, and Murren. For the amusement of his club members, he arranged a race in 1903, with skiing, skating, and tobogganing as the main attractions. While his race certainly marks a milestone in the history of downhill, it is not considered to be downhill's official beginning.

Two other historic races contend for the title of downhill's first official race. One took place in 1911, the other in 1922. According to Lund, it was a 1911 race that took place in Montana, Switzerland, that is considered to be downhill's first official race. It was organized by a British club and was called the Roberts of Kandahar Challenge Cup, presumably named after the club itself. This was the beginning of downhill racing, in which sheer speed was the goal. The Kandahar continues to this day and is now held in Murren, Switzerland.

According to Allen, however, it was Arnold Lunn who staged the first downhill race at Murren in 1922. Arnold observed his father's 1903 race and was inspired by it to form his own club in Murren and to experiment

with racing. Moreover, Arnold added obstacles in the form of sticks (which are referred to by some historians as flags, but today are known as gates) to the race course. Therefore, his race involved both speed and control (going around the gates) and, if not downhill's first official race, it can at least be considered slalom's first official race. In Lunn's day, it was speed, not style, that mattered in downhill. According to Allen, "early slalom competitors skied from one set of flags [or gates] to the next, fell down, got up and went on to the next

A skier stretches before a race at St. Moritz, Switzerland in 1926. Downhill races became popular in the early twentieth century.

obstacle."[28] Still, racers were penalized a certain number of points for stopping and for falling, although it is not clear how scores were actually tallied to determine a winner. Downhill and slalom races eventually became separate events, but their scores were combined to determine the winner, just as cross-country and jumping were considered combined events.

Downhill Racing Today

Although downhill skiing eventually separated from cross-country skiing to become its own sport, downhill skiing continued to evolve. Today, it features a variety of highly specialized events, each of which requires a specific set of skills. At one time, races involved mass starts, with all the competitors racing at once in what became a mad scramble for the finish line. Today, racers compete individually, and races are timed to determine the winner. They include downhill, slalom, giant slalom, super giant slalom, and the combined. These races are featured in skiing's two major events: the Winter Olympics and the World Cup.

Downhill Courses

Downhill racing involves skiing down a relatively straight course at top speed—as much as eighty miles per hour. It is a test of speed, bravery, and stamina. Early downhill races were called "straight races," and they were usually held above the mountain's tree line, where the course could be free of obstacles. Today, mountainsides are simply cleared of trees, stones, tree stumps, and other debris in order to set up a course.

Even with all this preparation, ski courses present skiers with particular challenges. These can include natural or man-made bumps, rolls, gullies, sudden changes of steepness, and varying snow conditions (such as snow that is warmed by the sun, which becomes sticky and slow, and snow that is cooled by the shade, which become icy and treacherous). Most courses include a jump and something known as a compression. A compression is a sharp descent followed by a rise, which the skier usually encounters at the end of the course when he or she is traveling at top speed. In the 2002 Olympic Games, the compression in the women's downhill course was referred to as a blind drop, and it represented the fastest and most technical section of the course—the one that would probably determine who would win and who would lose the race.

Downhill courses range from two to two and a half miles in length and are approximately twenty-two yards wide. Skiers must pass through a series of gates—actually just a flag on either side of the skier—on their way down the mountain. There are specific rules governing how a racer can maneuver around a

American Picabo Street flies in the air through two gates in the women's downhill race in the 2002 Winter Olympics.

gate. A competitor can knock down flags with his or her arms or shoulders, but both feet must pass between the two poles. Judges, known as gatekeepers, watch to see that the rules are followed. If both feet do not pass between the two poles, the skier is automatically disqualified unless he or she corrects the mistake by climbing back up the course and skiing through the flags properly. The ultimate decision for disqualifying a racer rests with a referee and jury. Because it is sometimes difficult for the gatekeeper to call a penalty, many arguments occur. The race referee and jury, after considering all reports from the gatekeepers, make the final decision.

The gates do not follow an exact straight line. Rather, they follow the curve of the mountain and are set at varying distances. The closer together the gates are, the more challenging the race. The women's downhill course in the 2002 Olympics featured thirty-six gates, for example. It also included a series of steep drops and falls, along with three major jumps. The course started at an altitude of 9,013 feet and ended at an altitude of 6,389 feet for a total vertical drop of 2,624 feet. Competitors were expected to descend the 1.95-mile run in about 1 minute and 42 seconds.

Downhill is the only Olympic event with training runs. For three days prior to the race, competitors participate in training runs to become familiar with the course. The race is one run. Time is measured to .01 seconds, and the person with the fastest time wins. The winning time for the 2002 Olympic men's downhill was 1 minute and 39.13 seconds on a 1.95-mile course. The silver medal time was 1 minute and 39.35 seconds and the bronze was 1 minute and 39.41 seconds.

Slalom

Slalom races evolved out of early downhill races, which were held above the mountain's tree line. Once the racers reached the tree line, they were no longer able to continue on a straight path. They had to navigate around the trees. Today, slalom racers face man-made obstacles. The obstacles (known as gates, which consist of two poles and a banner) are placed at specific distances along the course that are much closer than the gates a downhill racer must navigate. Rather than go through the gate, the slalom skier goes around the outside edge of the gate. The skill required in slalom is being able to turn quickly and change direction in order to reach the next gate. Skiers descend the hill in zigzag motion, at speeds of no more than twenty-five miles per hour in order to control their turns. It is a test of control and technique.

Slalom courses vary in length and number of gates. They range from one-fourth to three-eighths of a mile. The men's courses have a minimum of fifty-five and a maximum of seventy-five gates, and women's courses have a minimum of forty and a maximum of sixty. The distance between the gates cannot be less than 2.46 feet, according to FIS rules. The vertical drop for men's slalom races ranges from 196 to 240 yards. The vertical drop for women's slalom races ranges from 131 to 196 yards. In Olympic slalom events, each skier makes two runs down

Turning sharply on his edge, Austria's Stephen Eberharter navigates around the gates in the men's giant slalom.

two different courses on the same slope. Both runs take place on the same day. The times are added together, and the fastest total time determines the winner.

Memory is perhaps more critical in slalom racing than speed. This is because a slalom racer is allowed to test the course before the day of the race, but only for a limited time. Therefore, the skier must try to memorize the terrain, but not necessarily the position of the gates, as they are typically reset on the day of the race. At that point, racers are only allowed to examine the course by climbing up it, but not by skiing down it. Memory can make a difference between winning and losing. Olympic champion Jean-Claude Killy, for example, used what he referred to as a little secret to secure his win the Grenoble Games in 1968. He says: "I knew about the finish line. Early in the practice runs, I had realized that if I cut a sharp line just at the pole on the right, I could actually gain a couple of meters [a little over one yard]."[29] He was careful, however, not to test this theory during practice and risk giving away the secret to another competitor.

The Combined

Due to their popularity, downhill and slalom events were included in the 1928 Winter Olympics; however, they were only allowed to be included as exhibition matches, as they were not yet recognized as official sporting events. In 1936, they became official

 SLALOM GATE LINGO

The gates used in slalom racing can be configured in many different ways. However, there are two basic configurations from which most of the others stem. The first is open, in which an imaginary line drawn between the poles would be placed horizontally on the hillside. The second is closed, in which the imaginary line would be vertical (the same direction that the skier is traveling). The closed gate is also known as a blind gate, since it is more difficult for the skier to see. Robert Scharff, editor of *Ski* magazine's *Encyclopedia of Skiing,* describes the additional ways the gates can be set up.

From these two basic sets other combinations are produced. Two blind gates in a line are called a hairpin. Three or more are termed a flush. Two blind gates set apart with an open gater in between is an "H," or an offset "H" if any one pair is set out of line. All are tricky combinations meant to make it difficult when taken at maximum speed. A skillful course setter places the flags in such a way as to induce a skier to take chances in order to shave a fraction of a second off his time.

events, with medals awarded for the best combined times (for downhill and slalom). The combined involves one downhill race followed by two slalom races, in which the times are added together and the fastest total time determines the winner. The courses for the combined events are shorter than for the regular events.

The Winter Games resumed in 1948 (after being canceled in 1940 and 1944 due to World War II) with downhill and slalom as separate medal events, rather than combined events. The combined event was eliminated in 1952 and returned to the Olympic Games in 1988.

Giant Slalom

Giant slalom combines elements of downhill and slalom. It features the speed of downhill and the agility of slalom. The primary difference between slalom and giant slalom is that the gates are spaced farther apart, allowing for wider, smoother turns—and fewer of them. There are at least thirty gates set at least five meters apart. That way, the race is still a test of

good turning technique, but it is also a test of the skier's ability to travel quickly downhill. The number of turns is determined by the shape and incline of the course, not by the number of gates. This is because some gates do not require a change of direction. Therefore, the number of gates does not equal the number of turns, as it does in slalom.

The course is approximately one mile long. The vertical drop for men's giant slalom races is .25 to .37 miles. The vertical drop for women's giant slalom races is .18 to .29 miles. Each skier makes two runs down two different courses on the same slope. Both runs take place on the same day, usually with the first run held in the morning and the second run in the afternoon. The times are added together, and the fastest total time determines the

FACING THE FEAR

When downhill racer Picabo Street crashed on the slopes in 1998, it took two years for her to recover physically from the injuries. However, it took even longer for her to recover mentally. Before the crash, Picabo skied without fear. After the crash, she skied with caution. A sports psychologist gave her some principles for dealing with her new fear. What Picabo learned is that fear—when it finally sets in—never really goes away. She wrote about her experience in an article published in *Cosmopolitan* called "How to Confront Your Fears."

Slowly, as I put these principles into practice, my racing times started to improve. As I gained more confidence, I also gained perspective. I realized that I could have my fear on board with me and still succeed in spite of it. And I began to respect other athletes who had overcome major setbacks. Fearlessness can be wonderful—I would not have made it as far as I did if I hadn't felt so invincible before my accident. But it's the ability to work with your fear and rise above it that's truly heroic.

winner. The giant slalom became an Olympic event in 1952, the same year that the combined event was eliminated.

Super G

Super G stands for super giant slalom. It is the most difficult of the downhill races because of the speed and the challenging course. The course is hilly, with many twists and turns. The vertical drop for men's super G races is .31 to .40 miles. The vertical drop for women's super G races is .21 to .37 miles. Men's courses have thirty-five gates, and women's have thirty—spaced at least 27 yards apart. The course is shorter than a downhill course but longer than a giant slalom course. Each skier makes one run down a single course, and the fastest time determines the winner. The super giant slalom became an Olympic event in 1988.

Airborne at high speed, Janica Kostelic of Croatia balances her skis for a landing during the women's super G.

PICABO DESCRIBES A WINNING RUN

Downhill racer Picabo Street won a gold medal in the super G in the 1998 Olympic Games in Nagano. In an interview with Gabrielle Reece for *Women's Sports & Fitness,* Picabo describes the winning run. Her words reveal the difficult challenge an athlete faces in trying to establish the right attitude—a delicate balance between wanting to win and not caring at all.

I didn't have a care in the world that day. I wasn't even really supposed to be there, to be honest [because the super G is not my top race]. I didn't have anything to lose. It was perfect because I wasn't doubting myself, but I wasn't expecting anything either. Then I felt that adrenaline, that aggressiveness, because I realized, "Wow, this is race day; people are hammering it!" And it sent me up the next level, like, "this is not a phat little comfort zone for you; it's gold time. Let's go!" So boom! I take my run: rah, rah, charge. Hit the first five or six gates and I was just like, "Having one, whoo!" And I was just on it. Made my big mistake in the middle, just pissed myself off! And just boom boom boom for those next four gates, I gained so much momentum down the next pitch, around the corner, and then launched off that next jump, and I was like, "Okay, cool!" After I landed through the finish line, I saw I was 1.82 seconds ahead of the [next skier], and I went, "Whoa, I shouldn't have beat her by that much." I'm trying to talk myself out of it. All the other skiers were coming,

Picabo Street cheers after winning the 1998 super G.

bang bang bang, one right after the other, and I was waiting, totally waiting. Your job's done, nothing else you can do at that point, but you're so stressed out, so out of control.

Racing Equipment

Regardless of the kind of racing they participate in, all downhill racers need extra or specialized equipment in order to be competitive and safe. For example, to reduce air resistance, all racers wear skintight racing suits. In downhill and in super G, a racer's poles are designed to curve around the body, meaning that they are angled instead of straight. The purpose is to further reduce air resistance. Racers also wear helmets as protection in the event of a fall. The helmets are only allowed to cover the racer's head and ears. In slalom, a chin guard is added to protect the skier's face from being hit by the gates. Finally, goggles are used to protect the eyes. The goggles reduce the effects of weather, glare, and speed, but they do not influence aerodynamics.

Wax is as critical in downhill skiing as it is in cross-country skiing. Wax can be the determining factor in whether a racer wins or loses, because choosing the right wax for the particular snow conditions increases control and speed. For that reason, ski teams employ specialists called wax technicians. They can spend up to sixteen hours preparing a skier's skis before a race. Their tools include waxes, powders, brushes, and complicated formulas they keep in their head—or in a computer. The wax—which can cost up to five hundred dollars for a small block—comes in many varieties. Soft wax is used for warm weather and wet snow, and hard wax is used for cold weather. Some waxes are used as a base, and others are used as top coats. Fluorocarbon powder is added to the wax to reduce friction, and graphite is added to reduce static. Ski technicians labor away in what are known as wax cabins at the base of the mountains, where they study the conditions—even going so far as to view snow crystals under microscopes—and endlessly test their wax recipes.

Finally, there is one thing that all downhill racers must possess, something that no manufacturer can supply: attitude. The age of competition ushered in a new attitude toward skiing. As a sport, skiing was no longer simply a form of exercise—a way to improve mind and body—as it was once viewed by the cross-country skiers of Norway. Skiing became a challenge, both a physical and a mental one. Races were no longer tests of endurance and strength, but tests against time, against hundredths of a second to be exact. This kind of pressure demanded a certain mental toughness, which experts agree is the key to downhill skiing and to racing, in particular. Jean Weiss, who contributed a chapter on skiing to *Nike is a Goddess*, says just getting past the intermediate stage of skiing takes an aggressive attitude; becoming a racer takes even more. She says: "It's a mental game. If a skier doesn't have it in her head that she's going to win, she won't."[30]

Catching Air:
Ski Jumping and
Freestyle

SKI JUMPING IS among the oldest of the ski sports. It started as part of the cross-country tradition but, over time, evolved into a separate sport. Cross-country skiers revel in the great outdoors. They enjoy improving their physical fitness amid the beautiful landscape: the snow covered trees, the distant mountains, the blue sky above. Ski jumpers enjoy the great outdoors, as well. However, they enjoy it from a decidedly different perspective. Ski jumping is perhaps as close as humans will come to flying. In contrast to the cross-country skier trudging through the snow, the ski jumper launches from a jump and soars above it. A ski jumper looks down on the treetops, which probably seem small, as do the distant rooftops of the resort or village beyond.

Freestyle skiing, on the other hand, is the latest addition to ski sport. It appears to be part of the downhill tradition because skiers perform flips, leaps, and dancelike movements while speeding downhill. However, its origins can be traced to both the cross-country and downhill traditions, since it was started by both styles of skiers who wanted to add acrobatic elements to their routines, but not necessarily to competition. The ones who wanted to make freestyle part of competition were considered rebels, and from the beginning, freestyle was considered a separate sport. Freestyle skiing is highly entertaining. The speed, action, and risk of the aerial and mogul competitions create a sense of drama that always draws large crowds. While the two sports have different histories, they have one thing in common: being airborne.

The History of Ski Jumping

Ski jumping dates as far back as the first records of cross-country ski competitions, which include Norwegian military-held jumping contests in 1767. Ski jumping did not become a solo event until the 1860s. Before that, jumping was combined with other forms of skiing. For example, a downhill race might finish with a jump, or a cross-country competition might include several jumps. The first solo jumping competition was held in Trysil, Norway, in 1862. Cross-country's first major competition, the Christiania held in Norway in 1866, featured cross-country skiing and ski jumping as a combined event, though the events were separated later.

Ski jumping was part of the Winter Olympics from its beginning in 1924. The Norwegians dominated the sport for nearly three decades. From 1924 to 1952, Norwegian jumpers won all Olympic races as well as a substantial number of world championships. Throughout the

Anders Haugen, LeMoine Batson, Harry Lein, Sigurd Overbye, and John Carleton (from left), the first American Olympic ski team, pose for a photo in 1924.

1950s, skiers from Finland, Austria, Germany, and Czechoslovakia emerged as strong competitors, and, more recently, skiers from every country have become involved in the sport.

Another important event in ski jumping that is rooted in the sport's early history is the Nordic combined. Early in its history, ski jumping was combined with cross-country skiing. The Nordic combined features individual, sprint, and team events. The Nordic combined is considered to be one of the most challenging events, primarily because an athlete uses different muscles for ski jumping versus for cross-country, and in the combined event, he or she must learn to use both. Bill Demong, a member of the U.S.–Nordic combined team says: "You have to have enough endurance to handle the cross-country and enough explosiveness to excel at the ski jump."[31]

A Focus on Distance

Ski jumping is about distance. However, it is not exactly clear how the early ski jumps were performed. It is likely that jumping began when cross-country skiers encountered a drop or a gully and were forced to jump off it or over it in order to continue their cross-country trek. Perhaps early competitions were held in places where these conditions existed naturally (today, jumps are strictly man-made). Yet, historians do make a point of mentioning

that jumpers typically landed on flat surfaces, presumably because this enabled them to stop with ease.

Sondre Norheim was the first to jump onto a slope. This basic principle allowed him to cover more distance than previous jumpers. Therefore, Norheim is credited with discovering the essential and basic principle of modern jumping and, hence, is known as the father of ski jumping, among other things. (Norheim popularized the Telemark turn. He also was the first to rig his skis with a heel binding, which gave him greater control over his skis and allowed him to perfect his new technique.)

Norheim was also the first to set records in ski jumping. He is said to have jumped 98 feet and 5 inches—a figure that historians believe to be exaggerated. His pupil, Torjus Hemmestveit, held the world record with a jump of 77 feet and 1 inch in 1879, until it was broken by Olaf Tandberge with a jump of 116 feet and 5 inches in 1900. While the distances of these jumps have become part of history, historians note that the Norwegians were more interested in form—the style and grace with which they executed their jumps—than in distance. The focus on distance was actually an American invention.

Americans were thrilled by the distance records that ski jumpers could set. Ski areas were quick to construct jumps, and prize money was offered for the best

NORDIC COMBINED EVENTS

According to www.olympic.org, the official website of the Olympic Movement, the Nordic combined features three events, each of which involves a complicated combination of ski jumping and cross-country skiing.

Individual: Each competitor in the individual event takes two normal hill jumps during the first day of competition. Each jump is scored for length and style. On the second and final day of competition, each competitor participates in the 15 km cross-country event.

Sprint: The sprint event also is contested over two days, with the large-hill competition on the first day and the 7.5 km cross-country race on the second day. Unlike the individual and team events, the jumping portion of the sprint event is performed on the large hill and includes one jump instead of two. On the second and final day of competition, each competitor will compete in the 7.5 km cross-country event.

Team: Each team consists of four jumpers who take two jumps off the normal hill on the first day of competition. The team's score in the jumping portion is the total score of the eight jumps. The same skiers who participate in the jumping must compete in the 4x5 km relay, which is held the day after the jumping portion of the team event.

Japanese skier Daito Takahashi competes in the Nordic combined event in 2002.

distance. At first, the NSA (founded in New Hampshire by Norwegian immigrants in 1905) attempted to ban prize money. The Norwegians wanted to preserve purity of skiing—the notion that outdoor exercise benefited the mind and body. The organization also attempted to regulate the height of the jumps; however, jumping continued with no set standards. Therefore, the Americans simply constructed higher takeoffs and steeper slopes during this record-setting craze. Renowned jumpers—along with huge numbers of spectators—were lured to events such as the 1913 Steamboat Springs carnival where specially constructed jumps offered record-breaking possibilities.

By 1922, international standards for ski jumping were adopted, and in 1924 the ISF was formed, creating a governing body for skiing, including ski jumping. Guidelines for constructing jumping hills were finally created. For competition, ski jumps are built from scaffolding and erected on a hillside. The jump is angled according to the slope of the hill. Therefore, the skier is launched downward—following the downward slope of the hill—rather than upward. The jump is attached to the inrun, an incline on which a skier builds momentum before hitting the actual jump, at which point the skier is airborne. The landing—the spot where it is assumed that most of the competitors will land—is the steepest part of the hill. The halt is the end of the run, typically a

Skier Accola Rene launches off the end of a ski jump during the championships in 1923.

place where the hill flattens out and the skier is able to stop.

Today, ski jumping features three events: individual normal hill, individual large hill, and team large hill. The normal hill is 98 yards high. The large hill—used for both individual and team competitions—is 131 yards high. Competitors take two jumps, and the greatest total score determines the winner.

Distance, Style, and Landing

In ski jumping today, competitors are judged by the length of the jump, the style of the jump, and the landing. The length of the jump is determined by where the skier lands. It is usually a fixed and indisputable number. The style of the jump is a more complicated matter. Style refers to the appearance of the skier while "in flight," the time between launching off the ramp and landing on the ground. Style is a matter of personal taste and is judged by several referees. A successful landing is one in which the skier lands on his or her feet. However, landings are also judged on style. In certain regions, the height of the jump is also measured and factored into the overall score.

Ski jumping styles have evolved over the years—all in an effort to increase speed and the length of the jump. Early ski jumpers used the drawn-up style. They drew their skis up under them, which was thought to increase their speed and the length of the jump. As time went on, skiers changed to an upright style or a variation of it. They straightened their body and kept their arms flat at their sides, flying through the air like a missile, which proved to make them more aerodynamic. Some upright jumpers slightly adjusted the angle of their body or used arm motions in an attempt to better control either

STEVE McKINNEY DESCRIBES A JUMP

Ski jumper Steve McKinney of Squaw Valley, California, once described being in flight during a jump. His description appears in John Samuel's *The Love of Skiing.*

You concentrate on what is happening. You pole off from the start, one good push. Skate. Flick the tip of your ski like the tip of a condor wing. Drop onto your knees with your instantly streamlined body, piercing the air like the missile you are, driving yourself, taut and relaxed. Vibrations begin in the tip of the ski. At first it's a subtle shimmy. Then it rapidly encompasses both skis and body. The vibration crescendo is reached at about 110 mph. Then begins the quiet side of speed skiing, with the roar of the wind just behind. Smooth. Deadly if the mind slips. The steepest part comes at 128 mph. Then the test, the flat that has been rushing up like a huge white mass. Wham! White-black eye roll—involuntary gut-throat grunt. Thighs meet calves. Sometimes bum meets snow and gets toasted. Stand up at 100 mph into a banking turn with heavy lean. Apply brakes. Time-space warp. Back to the top, quick. Do it again, maybe better, maybe faster.

their speed or their direction. According to Matti Goksoyr, author of the ski jumping section of the *Encyclopedia of World Sports*, the Kongsberg bend is named after a group of skiers from Kongsberg, Norway, who were known for jumping with "a marked bend in the hip, arms out, and controlled arm rotations."[32] In this manner, they seemed to be able to steer their bodies, much like a rudder steers a boat. Others pointed their arms over their heads, as in a swim dive, cutting through the air like a swimmer cuts through the water. In all of these methods, the skiers kept their skis parallel. Today, skiers keep their arms at their sides and angle their feet inward so that their skis form a V, an idea introduced in 1986 by Jan Boklov of Sweden. This has proved to be the most efficient, aerodynamic style to date.

Throughout the history of ski jumping, skiers have landed in Telemark style, with bent knees and one foot ahead of the other. The landing is a controlled, graceful movement. However, the speed with which a skier lands can cause him or her to falter on the landing. Often, skiers have struggled to maintain their balance on the landing. They may lean to the side or fall backward, touching the snow with their hands or their bottoms, before straightening up.

The History of Freestyle

Like ski jumping, freestyle skiing involves being airborne. Yet, it has more in common with gymnastics than it does with ski jumping. That is because freestyle skiers are known for performing gymnastic flips, twists, and splits—all in midair.

Freestyle skiing is rooted in Europe and Scandinavia, but it blossomed in America in the 1960s. A number of cross-country and alpine skiers from Norway and the European Alps used the acrobatic maneuvers that are typically associated with freestyle skiing as part of their training routines. However, they did not display these techniques in competition. It was in the United States that skiing acrobatics were first seen in competition. Professional ski shows featuring freestyle skiing were held at the turn of the twentieth century. By 1950, people like Stein Eriksen, an Olympic skier from Norway who immigrated to the United States, had succeeded in popularizing freestyle skiing. The first freestyle skiing competition took place in 1966 in Attitash, New Hampshire, and by 1979, the ISF accepted freestyle skiing as an amateur sport.

There are three major areas of competitive freestyle skiing. One is stunt-ballet, in which the skier spins and performs gymnastic moves to music. Next is freestyle-mogul, a type of downhill racing. Last is aerial-acrobatic, made up of tricky stunts, including dives performed in midair. There are also group stunts, in which skiers perform a stunt like a back flip simultaneously.

The first World Cup in freestyle took place in 1980. It featured moguls, aerials, and ballet. So far, only two types of the freestyle skiing are featured in the Olympics: Mogul skiing became an Olympic event in 1992, followed by aerial skiing in 1994.

Mogul Skiing

Mogul skiing is a close cousin to downhill skiing. Yet, because mogul skiing involves skiing downhill over bumps and the occasional midjump trick, it is part of the freestyle category of skiing.

Although mogul skiing may have initially been inspired by the natural bumps in the terrain of a mountainside, mogul runs today are strictly man-made. The course is steep and the moguls (individual bumps) must be uniform and evenly spaced. The length of the run is between 755 and 855 feet, and the height of the moguls is up to four feet.

The skier's goal is to descend the mountain in as straight a line as possible. This is known as the fall line. However, the moguls are not necessarily spaced in a single line. Therefore, to follow a fall line,

American Shannon Bahrke performs a midjump trick in a mogul competition.

skiers must make continuous adjustments, turning perhaps toward the right to position themselves to ride over one mogul and then toward the left for the next mogul. Skiers bend at the knees and hips to absorb the impact of the bumps. They also keep their shoulders parallel to the finish line. In addition, skiers perform aerial maneuvers from jumps that are positioned at two points during the run. The first is one-third of the way down the run, and the other is two-thirds of the way down the run. Skiers are first judged on the following criteria: fall line, utilization of moguls, economy of motion (which means being fluid, appearing to ski without effort), absorption (bending of the knees and hips), carving action (which means turning), body position, pole plants, control, and aggressiveness. From this, an initial score is tallied. To that, scores for the height of the jump and for speed are added.

Aerial Skiing

Whereas mogul skiing is a close cousin to downhill racing, aerial skiing is a close cousin to ski jumping. Yet, aerial skiing features midair gymnastic routines.

As in ski jumping, aerial skiers take off from a jump. The jumps are built from dirt or from snow, rather than from scaffolding as in ski jumping. The jumps can reach thirteen feet high, with takeoff angles as steep as seventy degrees. The result is that

Aerial skier Tracy Evans of the United States squares out of a twisting flip, spotting for her landing.

the skier is shot up into the air to the height of a three- or four-story building. There, the skier begins to execute a series of twisting somersaults, all while plummeting toward the ground.

The skier is judged on three factors, which are then calculated based on the degree of difficulty of the particular jump. The first factor includes the takeoff, height, and distance. The second factor includes form, proper style, execution, and precision of movement. The third factor is the landing. Scores are added and then multiplied by the DD factor, a number that represents the degree of difficulty assigned to a particular jump.

Acroski

Out of aerial skiing has emerged a specialized form of freestyle known as acroski (formerly known as ski ballet). However, acroski is more closely associated with figure skating than with ballet.

Acroski involves a choreographed program set to music in which the skier performs jumps, spins, inverted movements, and linking steps. Equal points are scored for athletic ability (referred to as technical merit) as well as for artistic expression (referred to as artistic impression). In terms of athletic ability, the judges evaluate the degree of difficulty and the execution of the jumps (usually a minimum of three) and flips. Artistic impression is evaluated on creativity, variety, control, and the overall quality of movement. This freestyle sport is not yet an Olympic event.

Jumping and Freestyle Equipment Extras

Ski jumping is all about being airborne. Therefore, the equipment is designed for maximum lift. However, restrictions are imposed on certain equipment to avoid giving skiers an unfair advantage. For example, the thickness of jumping suits is regulated to limit the amount of air that can be trapped inside a suit, which would aid a skier's lift. Skis can be no wider than

FAT DON'T FLY

Ski jumpers generally believe that the thinner they are, the farther they will travel, a sentiment that prompted the phrase "fat don't fly." However, too much weight loss can seriously impact an athlete's health. According to a story by William Murray, a staff writer for www.nbcolympics.com, ski jumping officials are alarmed by the new emphasis on weight.

Alarm bells have also gone off in the offices of the sport's international governing body—the FIS—and the International Olympic Committee's Medical Commission. They have jointly commissioned a team of scientists headed by Dr. Wolfram Mueller of Austria to study the correlation between weight and the flight of the ski jumper at the Salt Lake Games. The team will gather enough information at the Games to run computer simulations. Based on what they find, Mueller says, recommendations will be made to the FIS for rule changes.

four and a half inches—a wider ski might enable the skier to catch more air, acting almost like a sail. Long skis can also provide lift. Therefore, ski length is determined by a formula that factors in a skier's height to ensure that no competitor has an advantage.

While many freestyle maneuvers involve being airborne, freestyle equipment is geared more toward ease of movement than toward improving lift. For example, there is no minimum ski length in moguls, but skis in aerials are usually shorter than the skier to allow for better movement in the air, which is calculated to the split second.

Freestyle, however, is credited with prompting a revolution in ski design and clothing. Granted, some equipment adaptations are designed to aid judging. For example, in moguls, skiers wear colored knee pads to enable the judges to better view the skier's knee control, which is factored into the skier's overall score. However,

Colored or designed knee pads, such as these "eyes," are common in mogul skiing to allow the judges to better assess a skier's knee control.

once freestyle became popular, experts such as John O'Brien, the director of the freestyle and mogul teams at Snowbird Resort in Utah and head mogul coach at Snowbird and Deer Valley, say clothing color changed to bright reds, oranges, and, for Americans, patriotic red, white, and blue combinations. He says: "Prior to that, people would only go skiing in things that were either gray or navy blue or black. [Freestyle] made a huge difference in the perception of skiing as a young person's sport or a more affordable sport."[33]

Finally, ski jumpers and freestylers wear helmets to protect themselves against injury, for these two sports involve death-defying stunts. Whereas cross-country races are tests of endurance and downhill races are tests of speed, ski jumping and freestyle have become tests of gravity or, more specifically, defying gravity. And, while it has been said that if downhill skiers do not have it in their heads that they are going to win, then they will not win, it can be said that if ski jumpers or aerial skiers do not have it in their heads that they are going to win, the consequences can be even more devastating. The mind is crucial to the sport, for a slip of the mind, as one jumper put it, can be fatal.

CHAPTER 5

Skiing's Legends

THE SPORT OF skiing has numerous champions. Olympic competitors hail from all parts of the globe, including Austria, Croatia, Finland, Germany, Japan, Sweden, and the United States. When ski racers win gold medals in the Olympics, they become stars in their own country. Yet, stardom for skiers is often short-lived—quickly replaced by the latest batch of gold medalists. The stars who stay in the public memory are those who stay in the public spotlight, both on and off their skis. They are the ones who go on to sponsor products, appear at events, or open ski resorts. In particular, they are the ones who exude a certain style and charm, a starlike quality that appeals to the media and to the public. In fact, while athletic ability wins medals, it is style and charm that wins hearts. These are the qualities that seem to be the true mark of legend or, at least, these are the qualities that people in the United States seem to appreciate most.

In the United States, the public finds its ski heroes in downhill and freestyle more often than in cross-country and jumping. While champions certainly exist in the sports of cross-country skiing and ski jumping, they tend to be dominated by skiers from Europe and Scandinavia. Finland's Matti Nykaenen won three jumping gold medals in both 1988 and 1992, for example, and Norway's Bjorn Daehlie earned double cross-country gold medals in 1992 and 1998. Yet, these two ski legends are little known among the general public in the United States. Another reason that Americans favor downhill and freestyle is that these sports are considered more glamorous than cross-country and jumping. People in the United States are drawn to the daredevil quality downhill and freestyle racers possess.

So, when *Ski* magazine revealed its list of the one hundred most influential people in the history of skiing in 1999, naturally downhill and freestyle skiers dominated the list. It also included inventors of equipment, the builders of resorts, the inventors of techniques, ski instructors, and team coaches—all of whom have contributed greatly to the sport. It is the skiers, however, who tend to live on in the public's memory. They are the ones who face the icy slopes, defy gravity, and win medals.

Gretchen Fraser

When downhill skiing made its official debut in the 1936 Games, the United States had no professional women's ski team. Instead, members of the Amateur Ski Club of New York made up the U.S. team, but all the medals were won by the more experienced European competitors. It was not until 1948 that Gretchen Fraser of Tacoma, Washington, won the first Olympic medals in skiing for the United States, capturing the gold in the slalom and the silver in the Alpine combined event. Not only was she the first female ski racer to win gold, she was the first

American—male or female—to win an Olympic medal of any kind in skiing. With her victory, European domination of the sport had been broken.

Gretchen grew up skiing on Mount Rainier. She moved to Sun Valley, Idaho, with her husband, ski racer Don Fraser, in 1936. They were both named to the U.S. ski team in 1940, but missed their chance to compete in the Olympics when World War II forced the games to be postponed. Gretchen kept herself busy, winning the U.S. national downhill and Alpine combined championships in 1941 and the U.S. national slalom in 1942, before deciding

Gretchen Fraser smiles after becoming the first American to medal in an Olympic skiing competition in 1948.

to retire from racing and teach skiing. Her husband coaxed her out of retirement and convinced her to try out for the 1948 Olympics. However, Gretchen was twenty-nine years old, much older than the typical Olympic skier at the time. She not only made the team, she won a gold medal in the special slalom and a silver medal in the Alpine combined (an event that is no longer part of the Olympics). According to Jean Weiss, who contributed a chapter on skiing to *Nike is a Goddess*, "She stunned the world, who had yet to see an American, let alone an American woman, do well in international competition."[34] Gretchen's historic win was truly an inspiration, for she was competing during a time in the history of sports when a female athlete was considered a contradiction in terms. Her success inspired more women to take up skiing and to compete. In 1960, she was inducted into the U.S. National Ski Hall of Fame.

Andrea Mead Lawrence

Andrea Mead Lawrence of Vermont was a member of the U.S. Olympic ski team in 1948—the year that Gretchen Fraser became a star. She was fifteen years old at the time. At the next Winter Olympics, held in 1952 in Oslo, Norway, Lawrence followed in Gretchen's footsteps. At the age of nineteen, Lawrence won not one but two gold medals: one in the slalom event and the other in the giant slalom event. It would be another twenty years

THE MAN WHO SKIED EVEREST

In the sport of skiing, there are those who demonstrate their daring on professional courses and those who choose another path. These skiers sometimes seek the treacherous conditions and slopes of remote places such as Greenland, the Haute Route in Switzerland, the mountains of Patagonia, and the North and South Poles. They are the extreme adventurers of skiing. One extreme adventurer recently became famous for attempting to ski down Mount Everest. According to John Samuel, author of *The Love of Skiing*, when Japanese super skier Yichiro Miura decided to be the first person to ski down Mount Everest, ski fans thought he would surely die.

Miura had equipped himself with a parachute and speed skis. His descent of 6,600 feet in 2 min 20 sec represented a maximum speed of 93 mph, but no-one who saw it on television is likely to remember it in such dry terms. Black as a beetle, darting for its life on a stark white backdrop, he was blown off course by a cyclonic gust. Those chattering skis, beyond mortal control it seemed, stayed on just long enough. He fell, hurt a hip, stopped short just before a crevasse, and survived.

Andrea Mead Lawrence carves a sharp turn through the women's slalom finish line gates.

before another gold medal was won by an American female racer in an Olympic Alpine event, and so far no other American racer (male or female) has won two gold medals in a single Olympic game. For this, Lawrence is considered one of America's most successful female racers. She was inducted into the New England Women's Sports Hall of Fame in 1999.

Like all downhill champions, Lawrence is remembered for her speed and her aggressiveness on the slopes. She is also known for a fall—one that has gone down in history as a famous Olympic moment. It occurred during her slalom race. She took the giant slalom race with ease, winning by an amazing 2.2 seconds. Her victory in the slalom was even more amazing, considering her first run was shaky: She fell after she missed a slalom gate, but got back on her feet and scrambled to regain her position, nearly falling a second time and losing 4 precious seconds. Her second run, however, was flawless. She beat the other competitors all by more than 2 seconds to capture the gold by a combined total of .8 seconds.

Following her ski career, Lawrence embarked on a second career. In her adopted home of Mammoth, California, she has spearheaded conservation efforts to stop overdevelopment of the region's ski area and to restore its lake. She also served four terms as a county supervisor.

Stein Eriksen

Stein Eriksen of Norway was also among the stars of the 1952 Winter Olympics. He won a gold medal in the giant slalom—which made its debut that year—and a silver medal in the slalom. Although his Olympic fame is based on downhill medals, Eriksen excelled in freestyle skiing and is said to have popularized the sport. Hence, he is considered the father of freestyle. He later became a highly regarded ski school instructor—known for both his style and his charm. Steve Cohen, author of "The 100 Most Influential Skiers of All Time," writes: "His flips helped spur the freestyle movement while his charm helped create America's first skiing sex symbol."[35]

Eriksen was born and raised in Norway—home of cross-country skiing and ski jumping. He was introduced to Alpine skiing by a friend of the family from Germany,

Stein Eriksen, considered the father of freestyle skiing, skis in the 1952 men's slalom.

who stayed with the Eriksens for several winters. He was also introduced to gymnastics by his parents, who thought the sport would help their slim son build muscle. A combination of gymnastics and skiing laid the foundation for his future freestyle success: He was at home both on the snow and in the air.

Following his Olympic win, he moved to Sun Valley, Idaho, in 1953, under an amateur contract. There, he trained with members of the U.S. ski team, who were in awe of Eriksen—they waited graciously for Eriksen to push off the mountain first before taking their runs.

At Sun Valley, Eriksen encountered conditions that were drastically different from what he knew back home. He actually had trouble making his way down the slope—that is, until he developed a unique turning method that allowed him to easily traverse the high-sided bowls of Sun Valley, during which he seemed to hang in the air and defy gravity. The turn involved a complicated weight shift and shoulder reversal—moves he perfected in gymnastics. Nicholas Howe, who witnessed the birth of the Eriksen turn, said: "For most of us, even the great ones, skiing seemed to be a muscular, difficult thing. What Eriksen did was something else. It was all lithe curves and delicate balances; it was the floating grace of a ballet dancer."[36]

Eriksen added a third title to his list of accomplishments—in 1954, he won gold in the World Championships in Are, Sweden, in the combined event—before deciding to retire from competition. Eriksen then entered the next phase of his career. He signed on as the head instructor of a ski school in Boyne Mountain, Michigan. There, Eriksen's reverse-shoulder technique soon rivaled the Arlberg system, which had been the cornerstone of Alpine ski instruction since 1902. Eriksen's method became the new sensation, and people flocked to Boyne to learn it, as well as to watch Eriksen, who by then was not only renowned for his gravity-defying turns, but for his flips as well. From Boyne, he moved throughout the United States to Heavenly Valley, Aspen Highlands, Sugarbush, Snowmass, and Park City—all of which were little-known resorts until Eriksen's presence made them famous. He opened Deer Valley, his home resort, in 1980. To this day, he is remembered as one of skiing's legends and by this motto: "Nobody Skis Like Eriksen."

Jean-Claude Killy

Jean-Claude Killy of France came onto the ski scene in the 1960s and virtually dominated the sport. He won the World Cup in 1967 and 1968—its first two seasons. At the Olympic Games in Grenoble in 1968, he swept the Alpine events, winning three gold medals.

From the time he was young, Killy was a rebel. He cut classes to ski. Killy says: "I couldn't breathe; I suffocated inside school. I was always called by the outdoors."[37] He dropped out of school at age fifteen, and at sixteen, he joined the French national junior ski team. What set Killy apart from his fellow skiers was the fact that he always took chances. This daredevil quality emerged early in his life and may have been fueled by emotions surrounding his mother leaving the family when Killy was young. Killy admits he was an angry youth, an anger that caused him to race aggressively, a style one *Sports Illustrated* reporter called hell-bent.

Sometimes, however, his hell-bent style caused him to fall. As a result, he rarely won a race. In fact, there were some races he did not finish, which lowered his ranking. He was ranked thirty-ninth when he finally won his first international race, a giant slalom, at age eighteen. Other times, illness and bad luck sometimes conspired against him, as in the 1964 Olympic Games, where he lost due to stomach problems and a lost binding.

By 1966, he was in top form. W.O. Johnson of *Sports Illustrated* writes: "In the 1966–67 season he was nearly invincible. Killy won 23 of 30 races, including all five World Cup downhills."[38] He considered retiring at the top of his game, but was encouraged to compete in the Winter Olympics at Grenoble in 1968, for the media exposure if nothing else. There, he reached the pinnacle of his fame, winning three gold medals and the heart of his nation.

In the years after Killy became famous, he became one of France's most powerful and influential people. He was instrumental in bringing the 1992 Winter Games to Albertville, for example. In addition to promoting the sport of skiing, Killy received contracts to endorse a number of products, becoming rich in the process. He then went on to start a ski-wear manufacturing company

on his own and several ski shops with his father and brother. Throughout his career, one thing has remained constant: He is devoted to the sport. For Killy, skiing was and still is a way of life. He says: "I always believed that skiing was something serious, that it was a way of living a whole life."[39]

Suzy Chaffee

Another heavily endorsed ski racer whose name became a household word is Suzy Chaffee. She started out as a downhill skier, becoming the highest-ranked American woman in Alpine competitions by 1967. Following the 1968 Olympic

Jean-Claude Killy (left) raises French teammate Guy Perillat's arm after winning gold and silver medals in the men's downhill event.

Games, she switched from Alpine to freestyle; however, freestyle was not recognized as an official sport by the ISF until 1979.

Chaffee was born in 1947 and was skiing by age two. Her father was a ski jumper and her mother was an alternate for the 1940 U.S. Alpine Olympic team. She was also trained in ballet and gymnastics, which gave her a distinct edge for freestyle skiing. When she made her switch from downhill to freestyle, freestyle had been considered an exhibition sport, not to mention a highly dangerous one (several competitors had suffered severe spinal cord injuries). Following her switch to freestyle, Chaffee established herself as the reigning freestyle champion. From 1971 to 1973, Chaffee won three consecutive World Championships—wins that were especially remarkable because she was competing against men (there was no women's division at that time). She was also the first to add music to her routines.

While her World Championship wins made her a legend, she is perhaps best known for the product endorsements that followed: She became a spokesperson for Chapstick and for Revlon's Charlie perfume. She was also the first woman to have a ski named after her.

Picabo Street

Suzy Chaffee was the best-known female skier in the United States until Picabo Street of Idaho came onto the ski scene. Street is considered the most high-profile U.S. racer today. She won a silver medal in the 1994 Olympics downhill competition and, after suffering a knee injury just fourteen months before and then suffering a concussion just a week before, she won a gold medal in the 1998 Olympics super G. She has also won two World Cup titles.

As with most champions, what initially set Street apart was her attitude. She claimed to have no fear on the slopes. When asked how she dealt with the fear that usually accompanies the dangerous sport of downhill racing, she replied, "I can't answer that because I don't experience it."[40]

All that changed after a second, more serious injury. Just one month after winning gold in the 1998 Olympics, Street was competing in the World Cup in Switzerland. In fact, she had planned to retire after the World Cup season. Then it happened: She crashed on the slopes during a run, hit a fence at sixty miles per hour, ripped her right knee apart, and shattered her left thighbone. Street was in intense pain, and the injuries forced her to take two years off skiing to recover. She set her sights on racing again because she did not want the crash to be the last memory of her career—in her mind or in the public's. Yet, before Street could ski again, she had to learn to walk. It took six surgeries and months of intense

PICABO'S BIG CRASH

One month after winning a gold medal in the 1998 Olympics in Nagano, Picabo Street suffered a crash during the World Cup finals that nearly ended her career. In an interview with Gabrielle Reece for *Women's Sports & Fitness,* Picabo describes the moment it happened.

The light was really flat. The jump was really big. The landing surface was a sidehill . . . so when I landed off the jump, I went to roll into my tuck and the ground deceived me. I thought it was less of an angle and it was more, so my right leg ended up underneath me. My [bottom] just dropped back and my hands were down and I went, Aaaahhhhh! And you've seen the rest: "Oh, God! Feet out to the right! No, feet out to the

left! Oh, God!" I kicked out and tried to spin hard enough to go parallel to the fence. Well I went in tips first. This leg came up, this leg went down and I went from 60 to zero in about two feet. This leg just blew apart; it had nowhere to go. I couldn't feel a thing, completely numb—"Oh my God, what happened? Is everything broken? Am I paralyzed? What's going on?" I just didn't know. And then I rolled over and both my legs just kind of dropped from my knees and I was like, Aaaaahhhh! I broke my leg at a diagonal and the bone displaced. So I had double femur bones sitting next to each other. It was nasty. I was just like, "Don't touch me! Get away! Somebody make the pain go away! Oh my God, this is brutal!"

Picabo Street soars above the snow. Street was seriously injured during the 1998 World Cup finals.

physical therapy before she was ready to ski. Her first race after the injury was the World Cup in 2000. It was an emotional time. Street said: "I stood at the starting gate with a knot in my stomach, my chest in a vise, and tears accumulating in my goggles."[41] She finished in thirty-fourth place.

Her return to the Olympics in 2002 was hailed as a heroic comeback, yet she had lost her edge: She no longer could ski without fear. She retired from the sport after the 2002 Olympic Games, where she finished sixteenth in the women's downhill. One reporter said it was a triumph just getting into the race. Street herself was not disappointed with her finish. While she may have lost her edge, she had held on to her positive, enthusiastic attitude. She said that she could look back on her career as a downhill champion with pride and that she was looking forward to returning to skiing—this time just for fun and recreation. Like Chaffee, Street became well known for the products she endorsed, including Chapstick and Nike.

Jonny Moseley

Freestyler Jonny Moseley was born in 1975 and began skiing at age three. His star quality was apparent at an early age: He was a Junior National Champion in 1991, 1992, and 1993 and was named Rookie of the Year by the FIS in 1994. In 1995, he began competing in World Championship and

 MIND OVER MATTER

Picabo Street spent two years recovering from her 1998 crash. But when she returned to the slopes, she found that her attitude toward skiing had changed. She was no longer fearless—a state of mind that wins races. She needed the help of a sports psychologist to overcome her fears. In her article "How to Confront Your Fears," which was published in *Cosmopolitan*, Picabo talked about what she learned from the sports psychologist and from the experience.

I learned how to tackle my growing trepidation. He taught me that you have to identify and categorize your fears into those you can control and those you can't. Then you have to set a limit on how much time you spend thinking about situations that are out of your hands. You can't just totally ignore your fear—it will keep nipping at you and will never leave you alone—but you can focus on controllable factors by replacing emotion with a concentration on the task you're trying to accomplish. However, it's not just a question of mind over matter. You also have to listen to your gut. If your fear is really intense, you need to walk away from whatever is causing it. You don't always have to be brave.

World Cup events. Moseley won Olympic gold in Nagano in 1998—the same year that Street won her second gold medal. His performance is remembered as freestyle skiing's most glorious moment. In particular, it was one new trick that stunned the crowd and gained him fame: the heli mute graber.

His trick was a twist on the traditional helicopter move, in which a skier crosses his skis in an X and spins like a top. Moseley added a midair grab—he grabbed his left ski with his right hand—and the heli mute graber was born. Moseley got the idea for the freestyle jump by watching a water skier, who was reaching under his right foot and grabbing his left ski off of the jump. Moseley first did the jump in a role for the movie *Breeze* and again during a precompetition practice at Breckenridge, Colorado. When he decided to add it to his Olympic repertoire, he made history.

American freestyle skier Jonny Moseley crosses his skis in a helicopter at the 2002 Olympics.

THE SKIER AS MEDIA STAR

In his article "Here's Jonny," Ken Castle of *Ski* magazine describes Johnny Moseley's rise to media stardom after his win at the 1998 Olympics. After Nagano, Castle says everyone wanted a piece of Moseley, thanks to his personality and charisma, not to mention his finely chiseled features and his knack for spinning one-liners. Castle says that Moseley was ready-made for television.

Moseley was put on a whirlwind tour that would make a campaigning politician beg for mercy. He appeared on the late shows ("Late Show with David Letterman" and "Tom Snyder"), the dawn patrol ("The Today Show," "Good Morning America" and "Live with Regis and Kathie Lee") and the afternoon shows ("Oprah" and "Rosie"). He got on a slew of TV sports specials, as a competitor in ABC's "Battle of the Superstars" (where he earned second place and a check for $20,000), as host of UPN's "Extreme World Records," and as a judge in a TV figure skating event. There was the obligatory handshaking with President Clinton, and the opportunity to throw out the first baseball of the season for the San Francisco Giants, who watched as he hurled a zinger across the plate. And, yes, that was Moseley in the McDonald's commercial that aired during the Games, a fortuitous pairing of "Big Air" and Big Mac.

Nicholas Howe, one of the authors of *Skiing* magazine's list of "The 25 Most Influential People," says that Moseley made skiing look effortless. He credits Moseley with sparking a renewed interest in skiing among the general public. He became a pop culture icon along the lines of Jean-Claude Killy. Howe writes: "He was irresistible and made the world again think of skiing as desirable, exciting, and cutting edge."[42]

The Hallmarks of Greatness

Each of these legends is remembered for their unique style and their unique contribution to the sport of skiing. Fraser, Lawrence, and Chaffee coupled daredevil attitudes with the desire to compete in an arena dominated by other countries and by men. Eriksen, Killy, and Moseley made skiing look effortless. Street skied without fear. All had a special quality—a certain charm—that made them stand out.

While style, charm, and unparalleled athletic ability seem to be the hallmarks of greatness among skiing's legends, Fraser, Lawrence, Eriksen, Killy, Chaffee, Street, and Moseley also embody the one quality that top athletes in every sport must possess: determination. They all had a determination that enabled them to conquer new ground. In the world of skiing, there will always be new ground to conquer and a new generation of daredevils willing to try.

Concerns for the Future

SKIING REMAINS A popular sport, fueled by the accomplishments of star skiers such as Jean-Claude Killy, Stein Eriksen, and Picabo Street, who have inspired so many to take up the sport. Still, there are three major factors that have emerged as concerns—or even possible threats—to skiing's future. One that has recently raised concern among experts in the industry is changes in climate. Experts warn that global warming is beginning to cause a decrease in snowfall and may one day eliminate snow altogether. While the general public may not be concerned with global warming, ski resort operators are beginning to discuss the future impact of this problem. A more immediate problem, however, is the growth of the ski industry, or more specifically, the impact this growth has on the environment. Clearly, the expansion of ski resorts is evidence of the sport's popularity. However, ski resort operators have been criticized by environmentalists, who believe that the continued expansion of ski resorts has a negative impact on the environment. So, environmentalists are urging ski resorts to stop expanding. One big reason that ski resorts are continuing to expand is the popularity of snowboarding. In fact, it appears that while the number of snowboarders is steadily increasing, the number of skiers is steadily decreasing. Just as global warming threatens to one day eliminate snow altogether, some think that snowboarding could one day render the sport of skiing a thing of the past.

Global Warming

Global warming is a distant threat, but some experts believe it warrants immediate attention. These experts argue that weather patterns are changing and that the climate in general is becoming warmer. It has been an issue discussed among scientists, politicians, and environmentalists for some time. But, because the effects of global warming will not be evident for many, many years, it is not a topic of major concern among the general public. It is especially not a concern to skiers.

Lately, however, global warming has become a topic of discussion among experts in the ski industry. This is because evidence is beginning to point to a reduction in snowfall; one study forecasted that Aspen, Colorado, would have a climate similar to Santa Fe, New Mexico, in one hundred years, which is too warm to maintain deep snow. Other evidence points to a shortening of the ski season in some areas, which experts attribute to global warming. A shortening of the ski season by a few weeks or even a few days due to global warming would have a tremendous economic impact because ski resorts would lose a significant amount of money.

Over the long term, journalist Peter Beaumont of the *Observer* says global warming could put an end to skiing altogether. Information such as this has prompted major concern among ski industry experts. Discussions about the problem and its future ramifications are under way (organizers of the 2001 North America's ski operators convention called global warming the biggest threat to skiing worldwide), but they are in the beginning stages, and at this point, no solutions to the problem have been proposed.

A young snowboarder flies high above the ground on the Nebelhorn Mountain in Germany.

Conservationists Are Against Ski Resort Expansion

While global warming may be the biggest threat to skiing over the long term, the biggest war being waged against skiing today has to do with the environment. While this does not necessarily present a direct threat to the future of skiing, it is among the industry's major concerns, primarily because environmentalists want to limit the expansion of ski resorts and, in some cases, close existing resorts.

As ski resorts continue to grow to meet skiers' demands, as well as to improve the resort's own profits, environmentalists are raising strong concerns. In order to keep their skiers happy and to attract new skiers, resort operators must not only maintain, but continually improve their facilities. This involves modernizing lifts, building better lodges, and continually making snow (according to Katherine Kerlin, an environmental writer, the Aspen Skiing Company uses 45 million gallons of water—some from local creeks—in one season). Improving facilities also means clearing forest areas for new trails, something that environmentalists fight against. It also means building more condominiums and vacation homes at mountain bases, which is sometimes done by resort operators as a way of diversifying their business. Other times, it is done by local developers. Regardless of who builds the homes and condos, environmentalists object, claiming

 WHY FIGHT FOR MOUNTAINS?

A key figure in the conservation of mountain ranges is Prince Sadruddin Aga Khan, who was born in Paris and raised in Switzerland. He has been instrumental in drawing attention to the environmental problems in the Alps. In addition to financing conservation and education programs, he founded Alp Action and was successful in cultivating sponsors such as Clarins, Timberland, and Proctor and Gamble for environmental projects in the Alps. He talks about some of the challenges—and unsolved mysteries—of conservation in an article by Richard Covington for *Smithsonian* magazine.

> Mountains have been woefully ignored on the global environment agenda, though they suffer the problems of acid rain, deforestation, erosion, overdevelopment and burgeoning tourism. They are arguably the most sophisticated air-conditioning machine imaginable; we still don't know exactly their role in global warming or the greenhouse effect. If the glaciers are melting naturally, does development of ski runs speed up the that process? If the glaciers become polluted, and the Alps are the water tower of Europe, what about water flowing into the Rhine, the Rhone, the Po and the Danube rivers?

that new development has a negative impact on the environment. Beyond creating noise, pollution, and congestion, new development threatens wildlife habitats.

Of particular concern to environmentalists are trees and wildlife, which are threatened by the destruction of their natural environment. In the highly popular Alps, for example, Richard Covington, author of "Drawn by Their Rugged Grandeur, Are We Loving the Alps to Death?" says 20 million skiers visit each year, creating eighty-mile-long traffic jams. Traffic, along with acid rain, has already damaged more than half of the trees there, and traffic is expected to double by 2010. He writes: "If the trend continues, according to a report from the International Center for Alpine Environments, one-third of existing woodland will disappear in 60 years."[43]

While the battle has made headlines in recent years, it is by no means a new issue. As far back as 1960, environmentalists were successful in halting plans by Walt Disney to create a giant ski resort between Los Angeles and San Francisco. More recently, an incident in Vail, the biggest ski resort in the United States with 5,400 skiable acres, grabbed the attention of both the media and the public. A group known as the Earth Liberation Front actually set fire to three buildings there in 1998 as a way of protesting the resort's

Vail Mountain's Two Elks restaurant smolders after the radical Earth Liberation Front environmentalist group set fire to it in October 1998, in protest of the resort's expansion plans.

plans to expand the resort by 520 acres—the biggest expansion of any North American ski resort over the past decade. Arson is certainly an extreme measure and a majority of environmentalists do not condone this type of tactic. They prefer to wage their battle through legal measures. One method, for example, is to classify a certain species of threatened wildlife as endangered, which gives environmentalists legal ground on which to defend the animal's habitat. The Alps, for example, are home to ibex, bearded vultures, lynx, and brown bears—all of which are considered endangered and are being protected by conservation groups.

There is evidence to suggest that this particular war may be resolved peacefully, however. Resort officials claim that environmentalists' concerns are taken into consideration during expansion. One resort boasted the number of trees it had spared in a newspaper advertisement designed to promote the expansion: "316,000 Lodgepole Pine, 193,000 Douglas Fir, 114,000 Englemann Spruce, and plenty of room to ski."[44] Some resorts are even establishing environmental departments. Katherine Kerlin, a writer for *E Magazine*, reports that the Aspen Skiing Company (which operates four mountains, three hotels, and fifteen restaurants in Aspen) was the first of several such organizations to establish an environmental department after the arson incident at Vail. More than

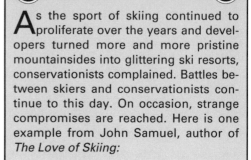

SKIERS VERSUS CONSERVATIONISTS

As the sport of skiing continued to proliferate over the years and developers turned more and more pristine mountainsides into glittering ski resorts, conservationists complained. Battles between skiers and conservationists continue to this day. On occasion, strange compromises are reached. Here is one example from John Samuel, author of *The Love of Skiing:*

> Mount Eniwa [in Japan], a virgin mountain of 4,000 feet, a pyramid of glittering birches, was manipulated [for the 1972 Winter Games] by 15,000 men, 850 bulldozers and six tons of explosives for two downhill races, the men's and the women's, and accoutred with two cable cars and a chair lift. As if by magic wand, it was then returned to its pristine state, as required by the conservation laws, within a few weeks of the end of the Games.

150 other ski resorts signed the National Ski Areas Association environmental charter, committing themselves to making environmental improvements on a volunteer basis.

Fewer Skiers on the Slopes

While global warming threatens to reduce the amount of snow and environmentalists threaten to reduce the number of resorts, there exists yet another danger to the future of skiing, one that threatens to reduce the most critical factor: the number of skiers. Experts say that the number of skiers on the slopes is decreasing simply because skiers are aging. A case in point can be found among local ski clubs. Jane Engle, *Los Angeles Times* staff writer, contributed a story to the *Times*'s travel section about travel packages available to ski clubs. Engle mentions that her own ski club is getting grayer and smaller. She also cites statistics that prove that skiers are aging: According to the National Ski and Snowboard Retailers Association, "Between 1990 and 2000, the median age of a downhill skier in the U.S. rose from 26 to 30.1."[45]

In the past, the graying of the ski population was of little concern. That was because there has always been a new group of young skiers to replace those who get old and retire from the sport. Today, that is not the case. *The Economist* reports: "The baby boomers who helped the industry take off in the 1960s are now older, and the number of young adults, who provide most new recruits, has declined."[46]

Perhaps the biggest reason that the number of new recruits has declined is snowboarding. Today's young people are drawn to snowboarding as an alternative to skiing. In her article, Engle says that the number of downhill skiers in the United States dropped from 11.4 million to 7.4 million from 1990 to 2000, while the number of snowboarders increased from 1.5 to 4.3 million. Today, the number of snowboarders on the slopes rivals the number of skiers and, in some cases, even surpasses the number of skiers. Nationally, snowboarders make up 43 percent of the people on the slopes on a given day. In southern California, the number is even higher. During a visit to a southern California ski resort over President's Day weekend, a *Los Angeles Times* sportswriter reported that snowboarders outnumbered skiers eight to one.

Despite the shrinking ski population, lift ticket sales have not been affected, since snowboarders need to get up the mountain too. Therefore, ski resorts will continue to flourish, as long as snowboarding continues to be popular. It does impact the sale of equipment and clothing—two key elements of the ski industry. However, manufacturers are usually able to adjust to—and even anticipate—market demands. Still, as the number of skiers declines and the number of snowboarders increases, it is possible that the sport of skiing will begin to fade into history, overshadowed by the newer, more exciting version of itself.

Snowboarding is, after all, just an adaptation of skiing—trading two planks for one, as one sports writer put it. The crowd at the 2002 Winter Olympics that witnessed snowboarders soar through half pipes can be compared to the crowd at Christiania that first witnessed the amazing

Three men smile as they hold their snowboards above their heads. Snowboarding's popularity is increasing.

jumps and turns of Sondre Norheim. In 1868, Norheim and his fellow Telemarkers ushered in a new era in skiing, just as the snowboard champions are doing today. What prompted both of these evolutions was a basic desire to try new challenges and the ability to develop the technologies and skills to succeed. Even ski legend Jean-Claude Killy was inspired to try snowboarding, which he says is the fastest piece of equipment yet on powder. In an interview with John Fry of *Ski* magazine, Killy said: "When someone invents a faster, better way to go down the hill, it is to be respected."[47] He further claims that snowboarding saved the ski industry, which many experts agree was on the decline. Therefore, as long as snow, humans, and imagination exist, skiing—in one form or another—will continue to exist.

Awards and Statistics

First Place Olympic Medal Winners Men's Cross-Country, 1924–2002

Olympic Games	Event	Nation	Name
Chamonix 1924	18 km	Norway	Thorleif Haug
Chamonix 1924	50 km	Norway	Thorleif Haug
St. Moritz 1928	18 km	Norway	Johan Grottumsbraaten
St. Moritz 1928	50 km	Sweden	Per Erik Hedlund
Lake Placid 1932	18 km	Sweden	Sven Utterstrom
Lake Placid 1932	50 km	Finland	Veli Saarinen
Garmisch-Partenkirchen 1936	18 km	Sweden	Erik August Larsson
Garmisch-Partenkirchen 1936	4 x 10-km relay	Finland	Kalle Jalkanen
Garmisch-Partenkirchen 1936	4 x 10-km relay	Finland	Klaus Karppinen
Garmisch-Partenkirchen 1936	4 x 10-km relay	Finland	Matti Lahde
Garmisch-Partenkirchen 1936	4 x 10-km relay	Finland	Sulo Nurmela
Garmisch-Partenkirchen 1936	50 km	Sweden	Elis Wiklund
St. Moritz 1948	18 km	Sweden	Martin Lundstrom
St. Moritz 1948	4 x 10-km relay	Sweden	Nils Ostensson
St. Moritz 1948	4 x 10-km relay	Sweden	Nils Tapp
St. Moritz 1948	4 x 10-km relay	Sweden	Gunnar Eriksson
St. Moritz 1948	4 x 10-km relay	Sweden	Martin Lundstrom
St. Moritz 1948	50 km	Sweden	Nils Karlsson
Oslo 1952	18 km	Norway	Hallgeir Brenden
Oslo 1952	4 x 10-km relay	Finland	Heikki Hasu
Oslo 1952	4 x 10-km relay	Finland	Paavo Lonkila
Oslo 1952	4 x 10-km relay	Finland	Urpo Korhonen
Oslo 1952	4 x 10-km relay	Finland	Tapio Makela

Oslo 1952	50 km	Finland	Veikko Hakulinen
Cortina d'Ampezzo 1956	15 km	Norway	Hallgeir Brenden
Cortina d'Ampezzo 1956	30 km mass start	Finland	Veikko Hakulinen
Cortina d'Ampezzo 1956	4 x 10-km relay	Unified Team	Fyodor Terentyev
Cortina d'Ampezzo 1956	4 x 10-km relay	Unified Team	Pavel Kolchin
Cortina d'Ampezzo 1956	4 x 10-km relay	Unified Team	Nikolay Anikin
Cortina d'Ampezzo 1956	4 x 10-km relay	Unified Team	Vladimir Kouzine
Cortina d'Ampezzo 1956	50 km	Sweden	Sixten Jernberg
Squaw Valley 1960	15 km	Norway	Haakon Brusveen
Squaw Valley 1960	30 km mass start	Sweden	Sixten Jernberg
Squaw Valley 1960	4 x 10-km relay	Finland	Toimi Alatalo
Squaw Valley 1960	4 x 10-km relay	Finland	Eero Mantyranta
Squaw Valley 1960	4 x 10-km relay	Finland	Eero Mantyranta
Squaw Valley 1960	4 x 10-km relay	Finland	Vaino V. Huhtala
Squaw Valley 1960	4 x 10-km relay	Finland	Veikko Hakulinen
Squaw Valley 1960	4 x 10-km relay	Finland	Veikko Hakulinen
Squaw Valley 1960	50 km	Finland	Kalevi Hamalainen
Innsbruck 1964	15 km	Finland	Eero Mantyranta
Innsbruck 1964	30 km mass start	Finland	Eero Mantyranta
Innsbruck 1964	4 x 10-km relay	Sweden	Karl-Ake Asph
Innsbruck 1964	4 x 10-km relay	Sweden	Sixten Jernberg
Innsbruck 1964	4 x 10-km relay	Sweden	Sixten Jernberg
Innsbruck 1964	4 x 10-km relay	Sweden	Janne Stefansson
Innsbruck 1964	4 x 10-km relay	Sweden	Assar Ronnlund
Innsbruck 1964	50 km	Sweden	Sixten Jernberg
Grenoble 1968	15 km	Norway	Harald Gronningen
Grenoble 1968	30 km mass start	Italy	Franco Nones
Grenoble 1968	4 x 10-km relay	Norway	Odd Martinsen
Grenoble 1968	4 x 10-km relay	Norway	Paal Tyldum
Grenoble 1968	4 x 10-km relay	Norway	Harald Gronningen
Grenoble 1968	4 x 10-km relay	Norway	Harald Gronningen
Grenoble 1968	4 x 10-km relay	Norway	Ole Ellefsaeter
Grenoble 1968	4 x 10-km relay	Norway	Ole Ellefsaeter
Grenoble 1968	50 km	Norway	Ole Ellefsaeter
Sapporo 1972	15 km	Sweden	Sven-Aake Lundback

Sapporo 1972	30 km mass start	Unified Team	Vyacheslav Vedenin
Sapporo 1972	4 x 10-km relay	Unified Team	Vladimir Voronkov
Sapporo 1972	4 x 10-km relay	Unified Team	Yuri Skobov
Sapporo 1972	4 x 10-km relay	Unified Team	Fyodor Simashev
Sapporo 1972	4 x 10-km relay	Unified Team	Vyacheslav Vedenin
Sapporo 1972	4 x 10-km relay	Unified Team	Vyacheslav Vedenin
Sapporo 1972	50 km	Norway	Paal Tyldum
Innsbruck 1976	15 km	Unified Team	Nikolay Bazhukov
Innsbruck 1976	30 km mass start	Unified Team	Sergey Savelyev
Innsbruck 1976	4 x 10-km relay	Finland	Matti Pitkanen
Innsbruck 1976	4 x 10-km relay	Finland	Juha Mieto
Innsbruck 1976	4 x 10-km relay	Finland	Pertti Teurajarvi
Innsbruck 1976	4 x 10-km relay	Finland	Arto Koivisto
Innsbruck 1976	50 km	Norway	Ivar Formo
Lake Placid 1980	15 km	Sweden	Thomas Wassberg
Lake Placid 1980	30 km mass start	Unified Team	Nikolay Zimyatov
Lake Placid 1980	4 x 10-km relay	Unified Team	Vasily Rochev
Lake Placid 1980	4 x 10-km relay	Unified Team	Nikolay Bazhukov
Lake Placid 1980	4 x 10-km relay	Unified Team	Yevgeny Belyaev
Lake Placid 1980	4 x 10-km relay	Unified Team	Nikolay Zimyatov
Lake Placid 1980	50 km	Unified Team	Nikolay Zimyatov
Sarajevo 1984	15 km	Sweden	Gunde Anders Svan
Sarajevo 1984	30 km mass start	Unified Team	Nikolay Zimyatov
Sarajevo 1984	4 x 10-km relay	Sweden	Thomas Wassberg
Sarajevo 1984	4 x 10-km relay	Sweden	Thomas Wassberg
Sarajevo 1984	4 x 10-km relay	Sweden	Benny Tord Kohlberg
Sarajevo 1984	4 x 10-km relay	Sweden	Jan Ottosson
Sarajevo 1984	4 x 10-km relay	Sweden	Gunde Anders Svan
Sarajevo 1984	4 x 10-km relay	Sweden	Gunde Anders Svan
Sarajevo 1984	50 km	Sweden	Thomas Wassberg
Calgary 1988	15 km	Unified Team	Mikhail Devyatyarov
Calgary 1988	30 km mass start	Unified Team	Alexei Prokourorov
Calgary 1988	4 x 10-km relay	Sweden	Jan Ottosson
Calgary 1988	4 x 10-km relay	Sweden	Thomas Wassberg
Calgary 1988	4 x 10-km relay	Sweden	Thomas Wassberg

Calgary 1988	4 x 10-km relay	Sweden	Gunde Anders Svan
Calgary 1988	4 x 10-km relay	Sweden	Gunde Anders Svan
Calgary 1988	4 x 10-km relay	Sweden	Torgny Mogren
Calgary 1988	50 km	Sweden	Gunde Anders Svan
Albertville 1992	10 km pursuit	Norway	Vegard Ulvang
Albertville 1992	30 km mass start	Norway	Vegard Ulvang
Albertville 1992	4 x 10-km relay	Norway	Terje Langli
Albertville 1992	4 x 10-km relay	Norway	Vegard Ulvang
Albertville 1992	4 x 10-km relay	Norway	Vegard Ulvang
Albertville 1992	4 x 10-km relay	Norway	Kristen Skjeldal
Albertville 1992	4 x 10-km relay	Norway	Bjorn Daehlie
Albertville 1992	4 x 10-km relay	Norway	Bjorn Daehlie
Albertville 1992	50 km	Norway	Bjorn Daehlie
Albertville 1992	combined 10 km + 15 km pursuit	Norway	Bjorn Daehlie
Lillehammer 1994	10 km pursuit	Norway	Bjorn Daehlie
Lillehammer 1994	30 km mass start	Norway	Thomas Alsgaard
Lillehammer 1994	4 x 10-km relay	Italy	Maurilio De Zolt
Lillehammer 1994	4 x 10-km relay	Italy	Marco Albarello
Lillehammer 1994	4 x 10-km relay	Italy	Giorgio Vanzetta
Lillehammer 1994	4 x 10-km relay	Italy	Silvio Fauner
Lillehammer 1994	50 km	Kazakhstan	Vladimir Smirnov
Lillehammer 1994	combined 10 km + 15 km pursuit	Norway	Bjorn Daehlie
Nagano 1998	10 km pursuit	Norway	Bjorn Daehlie
Nagano 1998	30 km mass start	Finland	Mika Myllylae
Nagano 1998	4 x 10-km relay	Norway	Sture Sivertsen
Nagano 1998	4 x 10-km relay	Norway	Erling Jevne
Nagano 1998	4 x 10-km relay	Norway	Bjorn Daehlie
Nagano 1998	4 x 10-km relay	Norway	Bjorn Daehlie
Nagano 1998	4 x 10-km relay	Norway	Thomas Alsgaard
Nagano 1998	50 km	Norway	Bjorn Daehlie
Nagano 1998	combined 10 km + 15 km pursuit	Norway	Thomas Alsgaard
Salt Lake City 2002	10 km pursuit	Spain	Johann Muehlegg

Salt Lake City 2002	15 km	Estonia	Andrus Veerpalu
Salt Lake City 2002	30 km mass start	Spain	Johann Muehlegg
Salt Lake City 2002	4 x 10-km relay	Norway	Thomas Alsgaard
Salt Lake City 2002	4 x 10-km relay	Norway	Anders Aukland
Salt Lake City 2002	4 x 10-km relay	Norway	Frode Estil
Salt Lake City 2002	4 x 10-km relay	Norway	Kristen Skjeldal
Salt Lake City 2002	50 km	Russian Federation	Mikhail Ivanov
Salt Lake City 2002	sprint 1.5 km	Norway	Tor Arne Hetland

First Place Olympic Medal Winners Women's Cross-Country, 1952–2002

Olympic Games	Event	Nation	Name
Oslo 1952	10 km	Finland	Lydia Wideman
Cortina d'Ampezzo 1956	10 km	Unified Team	Lyubov Baranova
Cortina d'Ampezzo 1956	3 x 5-km relay	Finland	Sirkka Polkunen
Cortina d'Ampezzo 1956	3 x 5-km relay	Finland	Mirja Hietamies
Cortina d'Ampezzo 1956	3 x 5-km relay	Finland	Siiri Rantanen
Squaw Valley 1960	10 km	Unified Team	Mariya Gusakova
Squaw Valley 1960	3 x 5-km relay	Sweden	Irma Johansson
Squaw Valley 1960	3 x 5-km relay	Sweden	Britt Strandberg
Squaw Valley 1960	3 x 5-km relay	Sweden	Sonja Edstrom
Innsbruck 1964	10 km	Unified Team	Klavdiya Boyarskikh
Innsbruck 1964	3 x 5-km relay	Unified Team	Alevtina Kolchina
Innsbruck 1964	3 x 5-km relay	Unified Team	Yevdoyka Mekshilo
Innsbruck 1964	3 x 5-km relay	Unified Team	Klavdiya Boyarskikh
Innsbruck 1964	5 km	Unified Team	Klavdiya Boyarskikh
Grenoble 1968	10 km	Sweden	Toini Gustafsson
Grenoble 1968	3 x 5-km relay	Norway	Inger Aufles
Grenoble 1968	3 x 5-km relay	Norway	Babben Enger
Grenoble 1968	3 x 5-km relay	Norway	Berit Mordre
Grenoble 1968	5 km	Sweden	Toini Gustafsson
Sapporo 1972	10 km	Unified Team	Galina Kulakova
Sapporo 1972	3 x 5-km relay	Unified Team	Lubov Mukhacheva
Sapporo 1972	3 x 5-km relay	Unified Team	Alevtina Olyunina
Sapporo 1972	3 x 5-km relay	Unified Team	Galina Kulakova

Sapporo 1972	3 x 5-km relay	Unified Team	Galina Kulakova
Sapporo 1972	5 km	Unified Team	Galina Kulakova
Innsbruck 1976	10 km	Unified Team	Raisa Smetanina
Innsbruck 1976	4 x 5-km relay	Unified Team	Nina Baldycheva
Innsbruck 1976	4 x 5-km relay	Unified Team	Zinaida Amosova
Innsbruck 1976	4 x 5-km relay	Unified Team	Raisa Smetanina
Innsbruck 1976	4 x 5-km relay	Unified Team	Raisa Smetanina
Innsbruck 1976	4 x 5-km relay	Unified Team	Galina Kulakova
Innsbruck 1976	4 x 5-km relay	Unified Team	Galina Kulakova
Innsbruck 1976	5 km	Finland	Helena Takalo
Lake Placid 1980	10 km	GDR	Barbara Petzold
Lake Placid 1980	4 x 5-km relay	GDR	Barbara Petzold
Lake Placid 1980	4 x 5-km relay	GDR	Marlies Rostock
Lake Placid 1980	4 x 5-km relay	GDR	Carola Anding
Lake Placid 1980	4 x 5-km relay	GDR	Veronika Schmidt
Lake Placid 1980	4 x 5-km relay	GDR	Barbara Petzold
Lake Placid 1980	5 km	Unified Team	Raisa Smetanina
Sarajevo 1984	10 km	Finland	Marja-Liisa Kirvesniemi
Sarajevo 1984	20 km	Finland	Marja-Liisa Kirvesniemi
Sarajevo 1984	4 x 5-km relay	Norway	Inger Helene Nybraaten
Sarajevo 1984	4 x 5-km relay	Norway	Anne Jahren
Sarajevo 1984	4 x 5-km relay	Norway	Brit Pettersen
Sarajevo 1984	4 x 5-km relay	Norway	Berit Aunli
Sarajevo 1984	5 km	Finland	Marja-Liisa Kirvesniemi
Calgary 1988	10 km	Unified Team	Vida Venciene
Calgary 1988	20 km	Unified Team	Tamara Tikhonova
Calgary 1988	4 x 5-km relay	Unified Team	Swetlana Nagejkina
Calgary 1988	4 x 5-km relay	Unified Team	Nina Gavriljuk
Calgary 1988	4 x 5-km relay	Unified Team	Tamara Tikhonova
Calgary 1988	4 x 5-km relay	Unified Team	Tamara Tikhonova
Calgary 1988	4 x 5-km relay	Unified Team	Anfisa Reztsova
Calgary 1988	5 km	Finland	Marjo Matikainen
Albertville 1992	15 km mass start	EUN	Ljubov Egorova
Albertville 1992	4 x 5-km relay	EUN	Ljubov Egorova
Albertville 1992	30 km	Italy	Stefania Belmondo

Albertville 1992	4 x 5-km relay	EUN	Yelena Valbe
Albertville 1992	4 x 5-km relay	EUN	Raisa Smetanina
Albertville 1992	4 x 5-km relay	EUN	Raisa Smetanina
Albertville 1992	4 x 5-km relay	EUN	Larissa Lazutina
Albertville 1992	4 x 5-km relay	EUN	Ljubov Egorova
Albertville 1992	5 km	Finland	Marjut Lukkarinen
Albertville 1992	combined 5 km + 10 km pursuit	EUN	Ljubov Egorova
Lillehammer 1994	15 km mass start	Italy	Manuela Di Centa
Lillehammer 1994	30 km	Italy	Manuela Di Centa
Lillehammer 1994	4 x 5-km relay	Russian Federation	Elena Vaelbe
Lillehammer 1994	4 x 5-km relay	Russian Federation	Larissa Lazutina
Lillehammer 1994	4 x 5-km relay	Russian Federation	Nina Gavriljuk
Lillehammer 1994	4 x 5-km relay	Russian Federation	Ljubov Egorova
Lillehammer 1994	5 km	Russian Federation	Ljubov Egorova
Lillehammer 1994	combined 5 km + 10 km pursuit	Russian Federation	Ljubov Egorova
Nagano 1998	15 km mass start	Russian Federation	Olga Danilova
Nagano 1998	30 km	Russian Federation	Julija Tchepalova
Nagano 1998	4 x 5-km relay	Russian Federation	Nina Gavriljuk
Nagano 1998	4 x 5-km relay	Russian Federation	Olga Danilova
Nagano 1998	4 x 5-km relay	Russian Federation	Elena Vaelbe
Nagano 1998	4 x 5-km relay	Russian Federation	Larissa Lazutina
Nagano 1998	5 km	Russian Federation	Larissa Lazutina
Nagano 1998	combined 5 km + 10 km pursuit	Russian Federation	Larissa Lazutina
Salt Lake City 2002	10 km	Norway	Bente Skari
Salt Lake City 2002	15 km mass start	Italy	Stefania Belmondo
Salt Lake City 2002	30 km	Italy	Gabriella Paruzzi
Salt Lake City 2002	4 x 5-km relay	Germany	Claudia Kuenzel
Salt Lake City 2002	4 x 5-km relay	Germany	Evi Sachenbacher
Salt Lake City 2002	4 x 5-km relay	Germany	Viola Bauer
Salt Lake City 2002	4 x 5-km relay	Germany	Manuela Henkel

| Salt Lake City 2002 | 5 km pursuit | Russian Federation | Olga Danilova |
| Salt Lake City 2002 | sprint 1.5 km | Russian Federation | Julija Tchepalova |

First Place Olympic Medal Winners Men's Super G, 1988–2002

Olympiad	Nation	Name
Calgary 1988	France	Franck Piccard
Albertville 1992	Norway	Kjetil Andre Aamodt
Lillehammer 1994	Germany	Markus Wasmeier
Nagano 1998	Austria	Hermann Maier
Salt Lake City 2002	Norway	Kjetil Andre Aamodt

First Place Olympic Medal Winners Men's Slalom, 1948–2002

Olympiad	Nation	Name
St. Moritz 1948	SUI	Edi Reinalter
Oslo 1952	Austria	Othmar Schneider
Cortina d'Ampezzo 1956	Austria	Anton Sailer
Squaw Valley 1960	Austria	Ernst Hinterseer
Innsbruck 1964	Austria	Josef Stiegler
Grenoble 1968	France	Jean-Claude Killy
Sapporo 1972	Spain	Francisco Fernandez Ochoa
Innsbruck 1976	Italy	Piero Gros
Lake Placid 1980	Sweden	Ingemar Stenmark
Sarajevo 1984	United States	Phillip Mahre
Calgary 1988	Italy	Alberto Tomba
Albertville 1992	Norway	Finn Christian Jagge
Lillehammer 1994	Austria	Thomas Stangassinger
Nagano 1998	Norway	Hans-Petter Buraas
Salt Lake City 2002	France	Jean-Pierre Vidal

First Place Olympic Medal Winners Men's Giant Slalom, 1952–2002

Olympiad	Nation	Name
Oslo 1952	Norway	Stein Eriksen
Cortina d'Ampezzo 1956	Austria	Anton Sailer
Squaw Valley 1960	SUI	Roger Staub
Innsbruck 1964	France	Francois Bonlieu

Grenoble 1968	France	Jean-Claude Killy
Sapporo 1972	Italy	Gustavo Thoni
Innsbruck 1976	SUI	Heini Hemmi
Lake Placid 1980	Sweden	Ingemar Stenmark
Saravejo 1984	SUI	Max Julen
Calgary 1988	Italy	Alberto Tomba
Albertville 1992	Italy	Alberto Tomba
Lillehammer 1994	Germany	Markus Wasmeier
Nagano 1998	Austria	Hermann Maier
Salt Lake City 2002	Austria	Stephan Eberharter

First Place Olympic Medal Winners Men's Downhill, 1948–2002

Olympiad	Nation	Name
St. Moritz 1948	France	Henri Oreiller
Oslo 1952	Italy	Zeno Colo
Cortina d'Ampezzo 1956	Austria	Anton Sailer
Squaw Valley 1960	France	Jean Vuarnet
Innsbruck 1964	Austria	Egon Zimmermann
Grenoble 1968	France	Jean-Claude Killy
Sapporo 1972	SUI	Bernhard Russi
Innsbruck 1976	Austria	Franz Klammer
Lake Placid 1980	Austria	Leonhard Stock
Sarajevo 1984	United States	William Johnson
Calgary 1988	SUI	Pirmin Zurbriggen
Albertville 1992	Austria	Patrick Ortlieb
Lillehammer 1994	United States	Thomas Moe
Nagano 1998	France	Jean-Luc Cretier
Salt Lake City 2002	Austria	Fritz Strobl

First Place Olympic Medal Winners Women's Super G, 1988–2002

Olympiad	Nation	Name
Calgary 1988	Austria	Sigrid Wolf
Albertville 1992	Italy	Deborah Compagnoni

Lillehammer 1994	United States	Diann Roffe
Nagano 1998	United States	Picabo Street
Salt Lake City 2002	Italy	Daniela Ceccarelli

First Place Olympic Medal Winners Women's Slalom, 1948–2002

Olympiad	Nation	Name
St. Moritz 1948	United States	Gretchen Fraser
Oslo 1952	United States	Andrea Mead Lawrence
Cortina d'Ampezzo 1956	SUI	Renee Colliard
Squaw Valley 1960	Canada	Anne Heggtveit
Innsbruck 1964	France	Christine Goitschel
Grenoble 1968	France	Marielle Goitschel
Sapporo 1972	United States	Barbara Cochran
Innsbruck 1976	Federal Republic of Ger	Rosi Mittermaier
Lake Placid 1980	Liechtenstein	Hanni Wenzel
Sarajevo 1984	Italy	Paoletta Magoni
Calgary 1988	SUI	Vreni Schneider
Albertville 1992	Austria	Petra Kronberger
Lillehammer 1994	SUI	Vreni Schneider
Nagano 1998	Germany	Hilde Gerg
Salt Lake City 2002	Croatia	Janica Kostelic

First Place Olympic Medal Winners Women's Giant Slalom, 1952–2002

Olympiad	Nation	Name
Oslo 1952	United States	Andrea Mead Lawrence
Cortina d'Ampezzo 1956	EUA	Ossi Reichert
Squaw Valley 1960	SUI	Yvonne Ruegg
Innsbruck 1964	France	Marielle Goitschel
Grenoble 1968	Canada	Nancy Greene
Sapporo 1972	SUI	Marie-Theres Nadig
Innsbruck 1976	Canada	Cathy Kreiner
Lake Placid 1980	Liechtenstein	Hanni Wenzel
Sarajevo 1984	United States	Debbie Armstrong
Calgary 1988	SUI	Vreni Schneider

Albertville 1992	Sweden	Pernilla Wiberg
Lillehammer 1994	ITA	Deborah Compagnoni
Nagano 1998	ITA	Deborah Compagnoni
Salt Lake City 2002	Croatia	Janica Kostelic

First Place Olympic Medal Winners Women's Downhill, 1948–2002

Olympiad	Nation	Name
St. Moritz 1948	SUI	Hedy Schlunegger
Oslo 1952	Austria	Trude Beiser-Jochum
Cortina d'Ampezzo 1956	SUI	Madeleine Berthod
Squaw Valley 1960	EUA	Heidi Biebl
Innsbruck 1964	Austria	Christi Haas
Grenoble 1968	Austria	Olga Pall
Sapporo 1972	SUI	Marie-Theres Nadig
Innsbruck 1976	Federal Republic of Ger	Rosi Mittermaier
Lake Placid 1980	Austria	Annemarie Moser
Sarajevo 1984	SUI	Michela Figini
Calgary 1988	Federal Republic of Ger	Marina Kiehl
Albertville 1992	Canada	Kerrin Lee-Gartner
Lillehammer 1994	Germany	Katja Seizinger
Nagano 1998	Germany	Katja Seizinger
Salt Lake City 2002	France	Carole Montillet

First Place Olympic Medal Winners Men's Moguls, 1992–2002

Olympiad	Nation	Name
Albertville 1992	France	Edgar Grospiron
Lillehammer 1994	Canada	Jean-Luc Brassard
Nagano 1998	United States	Jonny Moseley
Salt Lake City 2002	Finland	Janne Lahtela

First Place Olympic Medal Winners Men's Aerials, 1994–2002

Olympiad	Nation	Name
Lillehammer 1994	SUI	Andreas Schonbachler
Nagano 1998	United States	Eric Bergoust
Salt Lake City 2002	Czech Republic	Ales Valenta

First Place Olympic Medal Winners Women's Moguls, 1992–2002

Olympiad	Nation	Name
Albertville 1992	United States	Donna Weinbrecht
Lillehammer 1994	Norway	Stine Lise Hattestad
Nagano 1998	Japan	Tae Satoya
Salt Lake City 2002	Norway	Kari Traa

First Place Olympic Medal Winners Women's Aerials, 1994–2002

Olympiad	Nation	Name
Lillehammer 1994	Uzbekistan	Lina Cheryazova
Nagano 1998	United States	Nikki Stone
Salt Lake City 2002	Australia	Alisa Camplin

First Place Olympic Medal Winners Men's 90-Kilometer Individual, 1924–2002

Olympic Games	Nation	Name
Chamonix 1924	Norway	Jacob Tullin Thams
St. Moritz 1928	Norway	Alf Andersen
Lake Placid 1932	Norway	Birger Ruud
Garmisch-Partenkirchen 1936	Norway	Birger Ruud
St. Moritz 1948	Norway	Petter Hugsted
Oslo 1952	Norway	Arnfinn Bergmann
Cortina d'Ampezzo 1956	Finland	Antti Hyvarinen
Squaw Valley 1960	EUA	Helmut Recknagel
Innsbruck 1964	Finland	Veikko Kankkonen
Grenoble 1968	TCH	Jiri Raska
Sapporo 1972	Japan	Yukio Kasaya
Innsbruck 1976	GDR	Hans-Georg Aschenbach
Lake Placid 1980	Austria	Anton Innauer
Sarajevo 1984	GOR	Jens Weissflog
Calgary 1988	Finland	Matti Nykaenen
Albertville 1992	Austria	Ernst Vettori
Lillehammer 1994	Norway	Espen Bredesen
Nagano 1998	Finland	Jani Soininen
Salt Lake City 2002	SUI	Simon Ammann

First Place Olympic Medal Winners Men's
120-Kilometer Individual, 1964–2002

Olympiad	Nation	Name
Innsbruck 1964	Norway	Toralf Engan
Grenoble 1968	Unified Team	Vladimir Belousov
Sapporo 1972	Poland	Wojciech Fortuna
Innsbruck 1976	Austria	Karl Schnabl
Lake Placid 1980	Finland	Jouko Tormanen
Sarajevo 1984	Finland	Matti Nykaenen
Calgary 1988	Finland	Matti Nykaenen
Albertville 1992	Finland	Toni Nieminen
Lillehammer 1994	Germany	Jens Weissflog
Nagano 1998	Japan	Kazuyoshi Funaki
Salt Lake City 2002	SUI	Simon Ammann

Notes

Introduction: A Sport for the Body and Soul

1. Jean-Claude Killy, foreword. *The Love of Skiing,* by John Samuel. New York: Crescent Books, 1979, p. 6.
2. Dean Lunt, "Weather Hurts Ski Resorts' Earnings," *Portland Press Herald,* January 20, 1999, p. 1.
3. Andrew Bigford, "Skiing and the Environment," *Ski,* November 1999, p. 1. www.skimag.com.

Chapter 1: The Birth of Skiing: Cross-Country

4. Ted Bays, *Nine Thousand Years of Skis.* Ishpeming, MI: National Ski Hall of Fame Press, 1980, p. 1.
5. Peter Lunn, *Guinness Book of Skiing.* London: Guinness Superlatives, 1983, p. 16.
6. Nicholas Howe, "After All These Years, Nobody Skis Like Stein," *Skiing,* January 1990, p. 54.
7. Quoted in E. John B. Allen, *From Skisport to Skiing: One Hundred Years of an American Sport, 1840–1940.* Amherst: University of Massachusetts Press, 1993, p. 11.
8. Quoted in Allen, *From Skisport to Skiing,* p. 78.
9. Morten Lund, "A Short History of Alpine Skiing," *Skiing Heritage: A Ski History Quarterly,* Winter 1996, p. 14. www.skiinghistory.org.
10. Lunn, *Guinness Book of Skiing*, p. 12.
11. "Cross Country Skiing," NBC Olympics, February 22, 2002." www.nbcolympics. com.
12. John Samuel, *The Love of Skiing.* New York: Crescent Books, 1979, p. 76.
13. Lund, "A Short History of Alpine Skiing," p. 10.
14. E. John B. Allen, "Nordic Skiing," in *Encyclopedia of World Sport: From Ancient Times to the Present,* eds. David Levinson and Karen Christensen. Santa Barbara, CA: ABC-CLIO, 1996, p. 926.
15. Quoted in Lunn, *Guinness Book of Skiing,* p.16.

Chapter 2: The Downhill Craze

16. Lunn, *Guinness Book of Skiing,* p. 18.
17. Lund, "A Short History of Alpine Skiing," p. 6.
18. Samuel, *The Love of Skiing,* p. 13.
19. Lund, "A Short History of Alpine Skiing," p. 1.
20. Lund, "A Short History of Alpine Skiing," p. 9.
21. Lund, "A Short History of Alpine Skiing," p. 14.
22. Lund, "A Short History of Alpine Skiing," p. 9.
23. Samuel, *The Love of Skiing,* p. 16.
24. Samuel, *The Love of Skiing,* p. 17.
25. Samuel, *The Love of Skiing,* p. 58.
26. Lund, "A Short History of Alpine Skiing," p. 17.
27. Lund, "A Short History of Alpine Skiing," p. 1.

Chapter 3: The Age of Downhill Racing

28. Allen, *From Skisport to Skiing,* p. 99.
29. Quoted in W. O. Johnson, "A Man and His Kingdom," *Sports Illustrated,* February 12, 1990, p. 214.
30. Jean Weiss, "Rhapsody in White," in *Nike is a Goddess: The History of Women in Sports,* ed. Lissa Smith. New York: Atlantic Monthly Press, 1998, p. 139.

Chapter 4: Catching Air: Ski Jumping and Freestyle

31. Quoted in William Murray, "A Delicate Balance," Ski Jumping, p. 1. www.nbc olympics.com.
32. Matti Goksoyr, "Ski Jumping," in *Encyclopedia of World Sport: From Ancient Times to the Present,* eds. David Levinson and Karen Christensen. Santa Barbara, CA: ABC-CLIO, 1996, p. 912.
33. Quoted in Doug Miller, "Do the Evolution: Freestyle Skiing Rides the Wave of Perception," Freestyle Skiing, p. 2. www.nbcolympics.com.

Chapter 5: Skiing's Legends

34. Jean Weiss, "Rhapsody in White," p. 143.
35. Steve Cohen, "The 100 Most Influential Skiers of All Time," *Ski,* December 1999, p. 2.
36. Howe, "After All These Years, Nobody Skis Like Stein," p. 58.
37. Quoted in Johnson, "A Man and His Kingdom," p. 210.
38. Johnson, "A Man and His Kingdom," p. 212.
39. Quoted in Johnson, "A Man and His Kingdom," p. 212.
40. Picabo Street, "How to Confront Your Fears," *Cosmopolitan,* March 2002, p. 1.
41. Street, "How to Confront Your Fears," p. 2.
42. Nicholas Howe et al., "The 25 Most Influential People," *Skiing,* January 1999, p. 5.

Epilogue: Concerns for the Future

43. Richard Covington, "Drawn by Their Rugged Grandeur, Are We Loving the

Alps to Death?" *Smithsonian,* November 1993, p. 2.

44. Quoted in Chryss Cada, "Vail Environmentalists Lose Out to Ski Interests: Ecology Group's Tactics Turn Many against Its Cause," *Boston Globe,* January 9, 2000, p. 2.

45. Jane Engle, "Graying Membership Puts a Chill on Ski Clubs," *Los Angeles Times,* February 10, 2002, p. L2.

46. *The Economist,* "Winter Wonderlands," January 31, 1998, p. 1.

47. Quoted in John Fry, "In His View: Jean-Claude Killy," *Ski,* January 2002, p. 3.

For Further Reading

Books

Kate Haycock, *Skiing*. New York: Crestwood House, 1991. Part of the Olympic Sports series, this book discusses the origins of the Winter Olympic Games and the history of both Nordic and Alpine skiing.

Jean-Claude Killy and Al Greenberg, *Comeback*. New York: Macmillan, 1974. The story of racing great Jean-Claude Killy of France, who dominated the sport of skiing in the 1960s.

Andrea Mead Lawrence and Sara Burnaby, *A Practice of Mountains*. New York: Seaview Books, 1980. The story of one of America's most successful female racers, who at the age of nineteen won two gold medals, a record that still stands.

Arnold Lunn, *The Story of Skiing*. London: Eyre and Spottiswoode, 1952. Arnold Lunn of Great Britain pioneered the sport of Alpine skiing. His history is filled with personal anecdotes, which tend to favor British contributions to the sport. This book chronicles his years at the center of this new sport.

Russell M. Magnaghi, ed., *Seventy-Five Years of Skiing: 1904–1979*. Ishpeming, MI: National Ski Hall of Fame Press, 1979. A publication of the United States Ski Association, this book explains the development of skiing in America, primarily through anecdotes about the sport and those who influenced the sport.

Fridtjof Nansen, *Paa Ski Øver Gronland*. Oslo: H. Aschehoug, 1928. This is Nansen's original account of his crossing of Greenland, first published in 1890. It has been translated to English under the title *The First Crossing of Greenland*.

Luanne Pfeifer, *Gretchen's Gold: The Story of Gretchen Fraser*. Missoula, MT: Pictorial Histories Publishing, 1996. This is a biography of America's first gold medalist in Olympic skiing.

Picabo Street and Dana White, *Nothing to Hide*. Chicago: Contemporary Books, 2002. Library Journal calls this book engaging and honest. It is the story of Picabo's childhood and racing career told in her own fresh and informal voice.

Claire Walter, *Women in Sports: Skiing*. New York: Harvey House, 1977. Though many female ski champions have emerged since the publication of this book, it continues to serve as a useful resource. It covers some of the early champions of the sport of skiing, such as Barbara Ann Cochran, Annemarie Moser-Proell, Cindy Nelson, and Jana Hlavaty.

Websites

International Ski Federation (www.fisski.com). Known internationally as the Fédération Internationale de Ski (or FIS). Today 101 National Ski Associations compose the membership of the FIS. This website provides information on the Winter Olympics and World Championships in skiing.

United States Ski and Snowboard Association (www.usskiteam.com). USSA is the designated representative for skiing and snowboarding in the United States by the International Ski Federation and is recognized by the U.S. Olympic Committee as the representative for Olympic skiing and snowboarding.

Works Consulted

Books

E. John B. Allen, *From Skisport to Skiing: One Hundred Years of an American Sport, 1840–1940.* Amherst: University of Massachusetts Press, 1993. In addition to covering the history of the sport, the author discusses the origins of skiing as a form of transportation used by the military and the postal service as well as a popular form of recreation.

———, "Nordic Skiing," in *Encyclopedia of World Sport: From Ancient Times to the Present,* edited by David Levinson and Karen Christensen. Santa Barbara, CA: ABC-CLIO, 1996. This comprehensive reference book covers Alpine skiing, cross-country skiing, ski jumping, and freestyle skiing, including a description of each sport's rules, techniques, equipment, and origins.

Ted Bays, *Nine Thousand Years of Skis.* Ishpeming, MI: National Ski Hall of Fame Press, 1980. A thorough history of the development of ski equipment from the prehistoric ski to the modern ski.

Mark Bechtel, "Skiing," in *Sports Illustrated 2001 Sports Almanac.* Kingston, NY: Total Sports Publishing, 2000. Lists record holders in World Cup, World Championships, and Olympic events for the 1999–2000 season, along with a brief recap of events and people of note for that period.

Matti Goksoyr, "Ski Jumping," in *Encyclopedia of World Sport: From Ancient Times to the Present,* edited by David Levinson and Karen Christensen. Santa Barbara, CA: ABC-CLIO, 1996. A description of the origin, techniques, and rules of ski jumping.

Sigmund Loland, "Freestyle Skiing," in *Encyclopedia of World Sport: From Ancient Times to the Present*, edited by David Levinson and Karen Christensen. Santa Barbara, CA: ABC-CLIO, 1996. A description of the origin, techniques, and rules of freestyle skiing.

Peter Lunn, *Guinness Book of Skiing.* London: Guinness Superlatives, 1983. The Lunn family, particularly Arnold Lunn (Peter's father) and Henry Lunn (Peter's grandfather), was instrumental in establishing skiing as recreational activity and then as a sport. This book includes their contributions to skiing, as well as profiles of other key events and individuals.

John Samuel, *The Love of Skiing.* New York: Crescent Books, 1979. In addition to a history of the sport, this book offers how-to information, including a description of equipment, techniques, and popular destinations. The book also includes a foreword by Jean-Claude Killy.

Robert Scharff, ed., *Encyclopedia of Skiing.* New York: Harper and Row, 1970. Compiled by Robert Scharff and the editors of *Ski* magazine, all the material in this reference book originally appeared as articles in *Ski* magazine, an excellent authority on skiing.

Victoria Sherrow, *Encyclopedia of Women and Sports.* Santa Barbara, CA: ABC-CLIO, 1996. Brief account of the history of skiing and female record holders in the sport.

Jean Weiss, "Rhapsody in White," in *Nike is a Goddess: The History of Women in Sports,* edited by Lissa Smith. New York: Atlantic Monthly Press, 1998. This book covers the history and the female legends of every major sport. Each chapter is written by an expert in her prospective field. Weiss is the former senior editor of *Women's Sports & Fitness* magazine, as well as an avid skier and snowboarder.

Janet Woolum, *Outstanding Women Athletes.* Phoenix, AZ: Oryx Press, 1998. Features a list of all female record holders in the sport of skiing, as well as a brief description of skiing events and a history of the Winter Olympics.

Periodicals

Peter Beaumont, "Meltdown: Snowfall May Be Good in Europe This Weekend, but Global Warming Could Put an End to Skiing Altogether—And Soon," *The Observer,* January 14, 2001.

Chryss Cada, "Vail Environmentalists Lose Out to Ski Interests; Ecology Group's Tactics Turn Many Against Its Cause," *Boston Globe,* January 9, 2000.

Ken Castle, "Here's Jonny," *Ski,* September 1998.

Kim Clark, "Biathlon: Grab Your Rifles and Head for a Scandinavian Snowdown," *U.S. News & World Report,* January 28, 2002.

Steve Cohen, "The 100 Most Influential Skiers of All Time," *Ski,* December 1999.

Richard Covington, "Drawn by Their Rugged Grandeur, Are We Loving the Alps to Death?" *Smithsonian,* November 1993.

Bill Dwyre, "Still Changing: 1924 Winter Games Bear Little Resemblance to 2002 Model," *Los Angeles Times,* February 11, 2002.

The Economist, "Winter Wonderlands," January 31, 1998.

Jane Engle, "Graying Membership Puts a Chill on Ski Clubs," *Los Angeles Times,* February 10, 2002.

John Fry, "In His View: Jean-Claude Killy," *Ski,* January 2002.

Leigh Gallagher, "The Disney of Skiing," *Forbes,* December 13, 1999.

Rebecca Heino, "What Is so Punk about Snowboarding?" *Journal of Sport & Social Issues,* May 2000.

Nicolas Howe, "After All These Years, Nobody Skis Like Stein," *Skiing,* January 1990.

Nicolas Howe et al., "The 25 Most Influential People," *Skiing,* January 1999.

Steve Hummer, "Picabo Ends Her Magical Journey with Joy," *The Atlanta Journal-Constitution,* February 13, 2002.

Roland Huntford, "Hero of the Arctic," *Geographical Magazine,* April 1998.

W. O. Johnson, "A Man and His Kingdom," *Sports Illustrated,* February 12, 1990.

Katherine Kerlin, "Sustainable Slopes: Aspen Skiing Company Makes the Environment Its Business," *E Magazine,* November/December 2001.

Dean Lunt, "Weather Hurts Ski Resorts' Earnings," *Portland Press Herald,* January 20, 1999.

Gabrielle Reece, "Picabo: The Interview," *Women's Sports & Fitness,* November/December 1998.

Picabo Street, "How to Confront Your Fears," *Cosmopolitan,* March 2002.

Betsy Streisand, "Waxed to the Max," *U.S. News & World Report,* February 28, 2002.

Pete Thomas, "Historic Victory May Sweep Away 'Outlaw' Image," *Los Angeles Times,* February 15, 2002.

Internet Sources

Andrew Bigford, "Skiing and the Environment," *Ski,* November 1999. www.skimag.com.

"Cross Country Skiing," NBC Olympics, February 22, 2002. www.nbcolympics.com.

Morten Lund, "A Short History of Alpine Skiing," *Skiing Heritage: A Ski History Quarterly,* Winter 1996. skiinghistory.org.

Doug Miller, "Do the Evolution: Freestyle Skiing Rides the Wave of Perception," Freestyle Skiing. www.nbcolympics.com.

William Murray, "A Delicate Balance," Ski Jumping. www.nbcolympics.com.

Index

Picture Credits

About the Author

Alison Cotter earned a bachelor's degree in marketing from Syracuse University and a master's of fine arts in creative writing at California State University in Long Beach. She worked as a director of communications for Los Angeles's leading performing arts center and now specializes in marketing, public relations, and fund-raising as a freelance writer. Before settling into her career, Alison traveled throughout the United States, during which time she briefly worked at a ski resort near Santa Fe, New Mexico, where she learned to ski.